Beats Not Beatings

"An invigorating and thoughtful exploration, taking the reader to terrains not often visited from perspectives rarely heard. The biographies of the authors in this collection read like a wish-list of dinner companions one could only dream of."
—Dr. Michael Coyle, Professor, Department of Political Science and Criminal Justice, California State University, Chico

"A brilliant and compelling book that highlights the empowering and revolutionary nature of Hip Hop, a powerful medium that also highlights the corrupt and malicious criminal justice systems that serve the interests of the powerful. These essays make a profound contribution to the growing grass-roots movement calling for an inclusive, egalitarian, and sustainable future for everyone on the planet."
—Dr. David Nibert, Professor of Sociology, Wittenberg University

"It is refreshing, exciting and affirming to know that a collection of people have made the conscious decision to document hip-hop's resistance to the carceral state. A definite must-read for those interested in the relationship between carcerality and self-determination."
—Dr. David Stovall, University of Illinois at Chicago

"This book is an powerful ode to hip-hop. The essays form a 'scat' of hip-hop theory and application taking readers from the patrician streets of a falling Roman Empire to the queering of hip-hop in capitalist war zones. It's a book of public scholarship designed to resist academic repression and meet readers in the streets where critical thought turns into embodied action."
—Dr. Lea Lani Kinikini, Director, Institute for Research & Engaged Scholarship, University of Hawaii

"Since its beginnings, Hip Hop culture has always spoken truth to power, addressing state violence and surveillance. Beats not Beatings presents a novel anarchist counter criminology that foregrounds queer, criminalized, and deviant play through abolitionist impulses inherent in Hip Hop."
  —Dr. Mechthild Nagel, Professor of Philosophy and Africana Studies, SUNY Cortland

"Nocella et al., are magicians interlacing contemporary struggles to Hip Hop. The book's length and huge depth makes it a great read for people and folx that wish to carry on Hip Hop as a weapon for social change."
  —Lucas Alan Dietsche, Director, Save the Kids

Beats Not Beatings

Hip Hop Studies and Activism

Anthony J. Nocella II, Daniel White Hodge,
Don C. Sawyer III, Ahmad R. Washington, and
Arash Daneshzadeh
Series Editors

Vol. 4

Beats Not Beatings

The Rise of Hip Hop Criminology

Edited by
Anthony J. Nocella II

PETER LANG
New York · Berlin · Bruxelles · Chennai · Lausanne · Oxford

Library of Congress Cataloging-in-Publication Data

Names: Nocella, Anthony J., II, editor.
Title: Beats not beatings: the rise of hip hop criminology / edited by Anthony J. Nocella II.
Description: [1.] | New York: Peter Lang, 2024. | Series: Hip hop studies and activism, 2690-6872; vol 4 | Includes bibliographical references and index.
Identifiers: LCCN 2023051279 (print) | LCCN 2023051280 (ebook) | ISBN 9781433194184 (paperback) | ISBN 9781433194191 (hardback) | ISBN 9781433194153 (pdf) | ISBN 9781433194160 (epub)
Subjects: LCSH: Rap (Music)–Social aspects. | Music and crime. | Criminology. | Police brutality. | Hip-hop–Social aspects.
Classification: LCC ML3918.R37 B43 2024 (print) | LCC ML3918.R37 (ebook) | DDC 306.4/84249–dc23/eng/20231108
LC record available at https://lccn.loc.gov/2023051279
LC ebook record available at https://lccn.loc.gov/2023051280
DOI 10.3726/b21371

Bibliographic information published by the Deutsche Nationalbibliothek.
The German National Library lists this publication in the German National Bibliography; detailed bibliographic data is available on the Internet at http://dnb.d-nb.de.

Cover design by Anthony Nocella II and Peter Lang Group AG

ISSN 2690-6872 (print) ISSN 2690-6880 (online)
ISBN 9781433194184 (paperback)
ISBN 9781433194191 (hardback)
ISBN 9781433194153 (ebook)
ISBN 9781433194160 (epub)
DOI 10.3726/b21371

© 2024 Peter Lang Group AG, Lausanne
Published by Peter Lang Publishing Inc., New York, USA
info@peterlang.com—www.peterlang.com

All rights reserved.
All parts of this publication are protected by copyright.
Any utilization outside the strict limits of the copyright law, without the permission of the publisher, is forbidden and liable to prosecution.
This applies in particular to reproductions, translations, microfilming, and storage and processing in electronic retrieval systems.

This publication has been peer reviewed.

This book is dedicated to the youth that survived COVID-19 and the isolation during these trying times. This book is dedicated to all of those that died during COVID-19 and to those that lost loved ones because of COVID-19. Finally, this book is dedicated to those incarcerated during COVID-19 and who were sick and died.

Contents

Acknowledgments	ix
Foreword MIC CRENSHAW	xi
Preface CHANDRA WARD	xv
Introduction: Hip Hop History, Criminalization, and Justice MAURECE GRAHAM-BEY, DANIEL WHITE HODGE, ANTHONY J. NOCELLA II, AND ANTONIO QUINTANA	1
"No Homo": Hip-Hop, Homophobia, and Queer Justice ANDREA N. HUNT AND TAMMY D. RHODES	9
It's an Odd Future: Deviant Play and the Postmodern KENNETH R. CULTON	23
Thug Life: Hip-Hop's Curious Relationship with Criminal Justice andré douglas pond cummings	37
Música y Libertad VICTOR MENDOZA	67
Stop and Search: Representations of Police Harassment in British Hip Hop during the 1980s ADAM DE PAOR-EVANS	79
Legal Ambiguities and Cultural Power Struggles: The Moral and Legal Persecution of Rap in India LENARD G. GOMES AND ELLOIT CARDOZO	91

Afterword 105
 TASHA IGLESIAS

Contributors' Biographies 109

Index 115

Acknowledgments

I would like to thank Alison, Joshua, Dani, Jackie, and Naviya with Peter Lang Publishing. I would like to thank the co-editors of the book series Hip Hop Studies and Activism Dr. Daniel White Hodge, Dr. Don C. Sawyer, Dr. Ahmad R. Washington, and Dr. Arash Daneschzadeh. I would also like to thank the contributors who believed in this important ground-breaking book that provides the foundation to the field of Hip Hop criminology—"Mic" Crenshaw, Chandra Ward, Maurece Graham, Daniel White Hodge, Anthony J. Nocella II, Antonio Quintana, Andrea N. Hunt, Tammy D. Rhodes, Kenneth Culton, andré douglas pond cummings, Victor Mendoza, Adam de Paor-Evans, Lenard G. Gomes, Elloit Cardozo, and Tasha Iglesias. It is also so very important to thank all the people that took the time to read and write a supportive review of my book prior to it coming out—Dr. Michael Coyle, Professor, Department of Political Science and Criminal Justice, California State University, Chico, Dr. David Nibert, Professor of Sociology, Wittenberg University, Dr. David Stovall, Professor, University of Illinois at Chicago, Dr. Lea Lani Kinikini, Director, Institute for Research & Engaged Scholarship, University of Hawaii, and Dr. Mechthild Nagel, Professor of Philosophy and Africana Studies, SUNY Cortland. I would also like to that the many organizations and institutions that support me—Department of Criminal Justice, Salt Lake Community College, Academy for Peace Education, Institute for Critical Animal Studies, Poetry Behind the Walls, Save the Kids, Wisdom Behind the Walls, Utah Reintegration Program, Utah Tech Higher Education for Incarcerated Youth, Salt Lake Community College's Prison Education Program, *Peace Studies Journal*, *Transformative Justice Journal*, *Lowrider Studies Journal*, *Green Theory and Praxis Journal*, *Journal for Critical Animal Studies*, Dream Center Salt Lake Community

College, Dream Keeperz, Critical Animal Studies Society, Critical Animal Studies Academy, International Hip Hop Studies Association, International Hip Hop Studies Conference, Waterside Village, Utah Criminology Student Association, Syracuse Quaker Meeting, Utah Vegan Runners (York, Chris, Chris, Kate, Elke, Valerie) Salt Lake Community College Vegan Collective (Peter, Brandon, Alisa, Elisa, Mike and Caleb), Utah Alternatives to Violence Project, and Salt Lake Prison Letter Writing. I would like to thank my friends and family, MOM and DAD, Emma and Lucy, Ron, Ronnie, Lisa, Angelina, Joe, Camille, Connor, Logan, Chris, Kim, Kris, Nicky, Journey, Peggy, Bobby, Steve, Dennis, Dave, Rick, Beth, Dwight, Delano, Manny, Christine Camille, Brian Roberts, Jay G., Ben G., Jeremy, Emily Thompson, Gina Alfred, David Robles, Matt Wallace, Matt Holman, Chris Bradbury, David Bokovoy, Caleb Prusso, Whitney Harris, Roderic Land, Ashley Cox, Ashley Givens, Rita Branch-Davis, Mojdeh Kati Lewis, Adam Dastrup, Amy Woods, Cassandra Drollinger, Alexis Maurice, Antonette Gray, James Walton, William A. Calvo-Quiros, Liz Ramos, Brenda Santoya, Cha McNeil, Brenda Santoyo, Idolina Quijada, Julia Ellis, Chris Bertram, Brett Terpstra, Henry Milian, Stephanie Hoffman, Gavin Harper, Peter Moosman, Mojdeh Sakaki, Kamal Brewar, Cecile Delozier, Matt Sparks, Lauralea Edwards, Amber E. George, Nathan Reese Graham-Bey, Xris Macias, Antonio Quintana, Alisha Page, Lucas Dietsche, Alisa Garcia, Elisa Stone, Gary Cox, Jordan Halliday, Jay and Nick in Houston, Chelsie Joy Acosta, Marisol Burgueno, Fausto Mejia, Danielle Burnette, Cianna, Ellie, Gabriel Manzanares, Daphne Jackson, Priya Parmar, Reies Romero, Moneka Stevens, David Bokovoy, David Stovall, Alexandra Navarro, Amanda Williams, Aragorn Eloff, Carlos García, Jason Del Gandio, Carolyn Drew, Laura Schleifer, Les Mitchell, Mätita Nupral, Nathan Poirier, Peter McLaren, Sarah Tomasello Case, Richard White, Sarat Colling and Telis Gkiolmas.

Foreword

MIC CRENSHAW

In criticizing Hip Hop, we critique dominant culture. We hear a lot of talk about what is toxic in Hip Hop culture, the violence, misogyny, materialism. The settler colonial empire of the US has a violent and dynamic history that gave birth to the contradictions and conditions that shaped the circumstances, human experiences and environments from which Hip Hop manifested.

It's been said many ways, but Hip Hop as a subculture, is just a reflection of the larger society and its values. This form of modern cultural expression originated from ancient peoples experiencing and surviving colonialism and genocide in the so-called New World.

In its essence, Hip Hop is the concentrated, rendered, crystallized carbon building blocks of dominant western culture, forced through the prism of indigeneity of stolen, displaced Africans, colonized Native Americans and the creole derived from interfacing with European colonial settlers.

Internalizing race as a valid construct that separates people by ethnic, geographic, national, cultural, religious and skin color categories, we are giving dominant capitalist, heteronormative patriarchy power over our destiny and potential as human beings.

Interpreting race in our own self determined way, seeking liberation from oppressive dogma and deadly force gives us spiritual fortitude, guidance and orientation to something greater than what is imposed on us.

There is one human race, and we share the planet with other species. I recently read an adage that said, if humans were to disappear, other species would thrive, and, as a result of human civilization, all species may perish. Race being a dominant construct in the self-determined and collective identity of Hip Hop, is inextricably linked to sex, gender, sexuality, class and other demographic markers. If we criminalize the culture and people of Hip Hop and from whom Hip Hop emanates, we criminalize humanity. One thing I've come to value as a consistent element of Hip Hop in its purest form is that the authentic self will be held to account.

When the Hollywood paparazzi driven media hype that floods tabloids and social media platforms, and the major label, corporate financing of records and brands that artists represent is out of the picture, we are left with authenticity. There is substance before there is hype and we've grown comfortable with mistaking hype for substance. Let us remember that Hip Hop exists whether or not it is trending and that most participants in this culture are not rich and famous, they are contributing and bringing value to the culture because they love it and it is empowering. The commercial branding of lifestyle and aesthetic says through lyrics and imagery, that success is not just wealth, but opulence secured by deadly violence and willingness to do whatever it takes, whether selling dope, pimping, robbing or stealing to get it. This is an old trope that appeals to the ethos of the American Dream and rags to riches. To prove that we got everything from the mud at the expense of those who refused to support our grind, that paints a heroic effort that once realized is divine in its legitimacy.

In Hip Hop we are from and of the community and we are either valid or illegitimate to those who can hold us accountable for how we choose to express ourselves.

Hip Hop is criminalized because of its innate ability to hold power accountable. Let's hone and remember that.

If Hip Hop is thugs, misogyny, unfettered criminality, rape culture, addiction and toxic masculinity, it's only a mirror of the darkest elements of human behavior, standard in the ruling class and those who lead their institutions and enforce through military and police terror.

White supremacist patriarchy rules through military conquest, resource extraction and exploitation of human labor in the interest of private property that is protected by police through more deadly violence. Police departments evolved from slave patrols in the Southern US and enslaved African people and their descendants were the private property of slave owners. That legacy still informs police violence and terror visited on Black life today. Think about the George Floyd protests and the collusion between federal agents, the National Guard, the State and local police and the fact that Kyle Rittenhouse got away with murder.

Real Hip Hop like that emerging from the slums and ghettos, the after-school programs and community centers, globally, holds the potential of egalitarian diversity, meritocracy based on skill, apprenticeship and mastery, communication, expert expression, exquisite style and the highest potential for peace, love, unity and human evolution. I've seen this as elder B boys, B girls, turntablists, graffiti writers and emcees teach youth to be proficient in the elements of the culture in Germany, Russia, Cuba, Tanzania, Zimbabwe, Kenya, South Africa and Brazil.

The most oppressed and marginalized people have paid the highest price for the progress of Empire. Our labor, cultures, bodies, lands exploited have laid the groundwork for a machine driven by extreme narcissism resulting in apocalyptic destruction.

What do the oral traditions, the movement practices, the communal ceremonies and prophetic visions of the first peoples of Earth, holding on with resilience through resistance, have to say about the past, present and future? Could the youth and elders who are the offspring of these resilient cultures have access to an historic, current and futuristic way of communicating, being, celebrating and moving forward that is intrinsic to the foundational elements of Hip Hop? To me the answer is yes. Hip Hop has become the global language that it was in the Bronx in 1973 by finding its reflection and home on every continent and zone of the planet Earth where people dwell. Let's not forget to utilize our potential and capacity to hold power accountable and to continue to hold a mirror up to those who seek to evade what we've observed being done to us all. Let's hold that same mirror up to ourselves as we utilize art and culture with power, leadership and excellence to provide examples on how to heal and move forward with less violence, ignorance and destruction. Let us know better and do better throughout time and space with the means at our disposal to transmute pain and trauma into beauty with hope as a spiritual tool, crafting the work of healing, with confidence, because we have Hip Hop within us.

Our urban communities in the cities and our rural places of origin are the mines and the dumps as well as the pipelines to prisons and theaters of war. With the smallest percentage of the wealthiest hoarding more consolidated wealth than the whole of the human race combined throughout history, there is no denying that change is imminent, necessary. Do we expect the powerful and elite to engineer the coming changes in ways that redistribute their amassed wealth and seed peace, equity and prosperity for the masses? No, we know better. Do we expect armed struggle of the revolutionary sort to be the key to liberation of the oppressed globally? We've been conditioned to compete for dominance in manufactured social hierarchies for so long that random and sustained violence is predominantly horizontal and any organized efforts at armed political struggle tend to be isolated and vulnerable to asymmetric annihilation while simultaneously undermined by infighting.

We face a technological surveillance and anti-personnel military industrial complex, so overwhelmingly developed that there is simply overkill as a basic operating principle and a standard of warfare.

Preface

CHANDRA WARD

The most formative memory that forever changed my relationship and understanding of the power of hip-hop was in 1991 when the world finally got to see what Black communities have long experienced with police. On March 3, 1991, the infamous video was released on all major news outlets of a Black man named Rodney King being beaten repeatedly by four Los Angeles police officers. I was in middle school and listened to hip-hop that I was not supposed to listen to, but I was able to record NWA's "Straight Outta Compton" from my older cousin's extensive hip-hop collection. At the time, I regularly listened to anything from pop rap, like Salt N' Pepa and MC Hammer, to the Native Tongues and Public Enemy, to gangsta rap like Ice-T and NWA. The latter groups rapped about "mature" topics that I honestly didn't really understand but found attractive due to its hard-hitting beats and edgy lyrics. I listened to NWA's hit classic "Fuck tha Police" about police brutality against Black men in Los Angeles. At the time, I assumed that the artist's lyrics were a part of their posturing as studio gangsters. The depictions of police violence and the group's resistance to it seemed abstract, yet seductively rebellious to me. Then on that unforgettable day in March of 1991, I realized that Chuck D was speaking facts when he said, 'hip-hop is the CNN of the Black community.' In that moment, I saw the power of hip-hop as a vehicle by which to fight the power by amplifying marginalized voices. Hip-hop made me question the normative social order as tween. Hip-hop turned the mirror back on those in power who get to define who and what is deviant and exposed who in fact is the actual deviant.

Hip-hop, as a Black American art form, has almost always existed in relationship and proximity to criminalization. One of the founding fathers of hip-hop, Afrika Bambaataa, came to hip-hop after being a member of the Black Spades street gang in the Bronx. Out of the physical ruins of the Bronx, left behind from the ravages of white flight, disinvestment, and greedy landlords who literally torched buildings to the ground in order to collect insurance money, Black and Latinx youth created an art form, hip-hop. Just as Black bodies have been policed and surveilled since the first slave ship arrived on the shores of America, hip-hop, created from the descendants of enslaved Africans, would also be subject to scrutiny and even criminalization from those in power.

As hip-hop began to spread throughout the Bronx to the other boroughs, another element of hip-hop would come to be criminalized—graffiti. Graffiti was just another artistic expression of disaffected youth. Kids could gain a certain street stardom by tagging their names across makeshift canvases like subway cars. With kids making their mark on cars across the city, this drew the ire of officials in City Hall, who vowed to clean up New York. Cleaning up New York, among other things, meant implementing a penal crackdown on graffiti and graffiti artists. The surveillance of Black and Brown bodies was now extended through the criminalization of graffiti. The subculture that emerged from the Bronx, now received the label of deviant in the eyes of general public. This label would continue to be applied to hip-hop in the collective consciousness of many Americans throughout the subsequent decades. Hip-hop would become a part of a seemingly "natural" constellation of deviance that included Blackness and the very loaded term, "urban." In a not too unsurprising turn of events, graffiti drew the attention of the uptown, white, elite art scene. Soon, "deviant" graffiti artists were turned "legit" by those who possess the power to assign social labels—whites. Street artists, as they were now referred to, such as Lee Quinones, Lady Pink, and most notably Jean Michel Basquiat were embraced as the new exotic thing in art galleries uptown. Once graffiti was contained within the walls of art galleries and turned into a commodity by rich, white art collectors, the same art was no longer considered deviant. This act of controlling elements of hip-hop for commodification and consumption continued as hip hop began to make its way to the mainstream.

As hip-hop continued to rise in popularity in the late 1980s and early 1990s, this popularity did not shield it from attacks at the highest levels of the U.S government. Some of the very same artists whose music awoke me in middle school, were now the targets of criminalization by the state. This began in 1985 when then, former Second Lady, wife of former Vice President Al Gore, formed the media watchdog group Parent's Music Resource Center. The group was able to create a moral panic around music lyrics and was successful in getting record companies to put a "parental advisory" label on music that contained explicit lyrics. However, it did not stop there. Record store employees received anywhere from fines to imprisonment for selling music that contained the parental advisory label to kids deemed underage. While many artists were targeted by this group, hip-hop artists were fined and even jailed after performing lyrics labeled as obscene. Most notably, members of the Miami-based rap group 2-Live Crew were arrested after a performance in Florida. A court passed down a judgment that one of the group's albums was obscene leading the court to ban the album from being sold anywhere in the U.S! After the members were arrested for performing, a record store employee was also arrested for selling the album. Their case went to trial where all parties were eventually acquitted.

Perhaps coming full circle, the group that allowed me to make connections between personal experience and social structure, indeed perhaps laying the groundwork for my becoming a sociologist, NWA faced its own battle from the highest levels of government around the same time as 2-Live Crew. In 1989, following the release of "Fuck tha Police," the Federal Bureau of Investigation (FBI) sent a letter to NWA's record label, Priority Records, condemning the group's music and receiving condemnation from the law enforcement community writ large.

Hip-hop's relationship with definitions of deviance, having the deviant label applied to the genre, the culture, and the artists is exactly what makes the essays in this book a refreshing addition to the literature on hip-hop and criminology. "Beats Not Beatings: The Rise of Hip Hop Criminology" engages with the many power dynamics that has shaped the culture producing these global phenomena called hip-hop, just like hip-hop shaped my socio-political views at the impressionable age of twelve.

Introduction: Hip Hop History, Criminalization, and Justice

MAURECE GRAHAM-BEY, DANIEL WHITE HODGE, ANTHONY J. NOCELLA II, AND ANTONIO QUINTANA

Introduction

For many, Hip Hop is a discourse vehicle, which echoes the concerns, anger, hate, love, pain, hope, vision, anxiety, desire, and joy which had gone unheard in the media (Forman 2007. Hip Hop is, as Chuck D once said, "our CNN." It is a voice of the marginalized, oppressed, and disenfranchised, which speaks their story to the world. That voice, which emerged in the 1970s first out of Black youth in the Bronx, New York provides a place at the social table to create space for the turmoil being lived out across America's "hoods" (Chang 2005; Rose 1994).

I, Hodge, was at an early age when I was first introduced to the culture of Hip Hop. The rhythm and lyrical flow were simply awe inspiring. Moreover, I saw myself in the music itself; my identity, my struggle, my racialized life journey, all there in musical form. By the time I was a teenager growing up in the Bay Area, an entire West Coast genre had been formed and a type of consciousness befell me. Artists who emerged from this moment began to give voice to the universal struggle many Black and PoC face daily. I knew then, this was more than just "music;" this was a movement.

Through Hip Hop, one was able to realize the reprehensible common experience happening in the urban centers, and that one was not alone in that experience; it was a narrative that needed explaining and needed to be told (Hodge 2010; Hodge, Sawyer III, Nocella II, & Washington 2020). It was a narrative which would lay the ground for postmodern and post-soul resistance for decades to come. Hip Hop was, and still is, a way to construct thought, question authority, and express anger, frustration, hate, revolutionary worldviews, and rebellious spirits (Prior 2012).

Even so though, Black and Latinx bodies who speak truth to power, are educated, and refuse to bow to white colonization are always a danger to the U.S. establishment of society. In that sense, Hip Hop culture is, as many rappers have exclaimed, "America's most wanted." Why is that, however? Rap music and Hip Hop culture were not the first to challenge systems of authority or create music that are societally and politically centered on equity. The 1950s was full of artists such as Elvis, Johnny Cash, Roy Orbison…all had a sense of "rebellion" about them in style, prose, art, and premise. The 1960s would of course see the rise of "Hippie Culture" and a complete refusal of societal norms; one can imagine the capstone of this refusal when in 1969 Woodstock ferried a crowd of young people pushing against established mores, beliefs, and traditions. Woodstock was not a crowd of "Boomers" attempting to fit in or create some nostalgia of the U.S. being "great." No, quite the contrary. Music was at the center of it and established a sense of rebellion— especially in popular culture. Yes, one can agree that there were arrests made, pushback from adults, and a terror for the future of the U.S. by those in power. Yet, arguably, none of them evoked the anger, ire, and disgust that Hip Hop has over the past thirty-five years. The image of the thug, gangbanger, hoodlum, and/ or criminal is a known trope associated with Hip Hop culture (Perry 2004). Moreover, the terminology of "gangster rap" was not something the culture developed but record executives anxious to categorize this new trend during the mid-1980s. This would go on to be popularized in the media as Black and Latinx youth who bore Jheri curls, hooded sweatshirts, and dark colored clothing as a signature for violence, drug sales, and all things evil—the loud rumbling bass emanating from vehicles did not help any either and often came with a criminalized ideology (Boyd 2004). But let us take a step back and look into the culture to explore what makes Hip Hop such a criminalized genre for so many.

Hip Hop founded in the 1970s in Bronx, New York, USA by Black and Latinx youth was influenced by Jamaican music and culture, because of the founder DJ Kool Herc, a Jamaican-American, who was born in Kngston, Jamaica. DJ Kool Herc was most known for founding Hip Hop through his loud fun grass-roots low budget street and house parties. Hip Hop with no money, but creativity in their pocket, has become the fastest growing youth cultures in the world with a net worth over ten billion US dollars. This powerful and influential culture influences all parts of the global society

Introduction: Hip Hop History, Criminalization   3

from politics and economics to religion and identity. The story of Hip Hop and Hip Hop studies would not be authentic if repression, oppression, and suppression were not mentioned toward the economically disadvantaged and Black, Indigenous, People of Color (BIPOC) communities (Ball 2011; Nocella II, Best, & McLaren 2010). Hip Hop spoke out about state sponsored violence and terrorism, referred by liberals as— police brutality, mass incarceration, gentrification, and the war on drugs. Police brutality if almost never prosecuted and found guilty is by definition supported and sponsored by the state to physically control and cause fear in the minds of those they oppose. Mass incarceration is to say that incarceration by itself is not wrong, but rather too many people incarcerated is not efficient for the reason that taking too many oppressed out of their community causes a burden to those in power, thus forcing those in power to develop a welfare charity industry to those they oppress (Davis 2003; Alexander 2012). This welfare charity industry is from those in power's perspective seeping into all parts of society, thus forcing gentrification to emerge and driving the welfare charity industry out of communities and into the most outer bounds of human civilization so they are out of sight and out of mind. Finally, the war on drugs is still in place and entrenched into all parts of society because of the hegemonic authoritarian tyrannical mega-force is striving to foster a global state of human docility for the ultimate efficient consumer and producer corporate normalcy model, where every thought and identity is controlled.

Hip Hop transcends the mediated tropes of sexualized PoC bodies only yammering for money, fame, fortune, and to "be the best." Hip Hop is much more than tattoos, arpeggiated high hats and snares, gold chains, fancy grills, and baggy pants (albeit that was in the late 90's) (Rose 2008). No, Hip Hop is a culture; a lifestyle; something that we must take into strong consideration and begin to not just analyze it for lyrical purposes, but begin to ask, what does and can Hip Hop offer theologically and how might it inform our own lives?

Hip Hop is larger than the radio, commercialized artists, and record industry branding. It is a culture, a people, a movement, a growing community of people that live, breathe, eat, love, hate, and work just as anyone else does (Dyson 2001). Hip Hop cannot be easily understood or defined (Forman 2007). It is complex and full of narratives that would blow away even the strongest anthropologist. Hip Hop, in the words of KRS-One, is "something that is being lived" (Parmar 2009).

It is here Hip Hop resists, revolts, and rebels for liberation, freedom, autonomy, and self-determination since its birth in the Bronx. Hip Hop like anarchism were stigmatized for their ability, commitment, and articulation on the subjects of justice, crime, harm, violence, and accountability. Hip Hop and anarchism were always criminological theories, but the reason they were not valued and accepted were they were critical and calling those that were enforcing the laws the criminals, rather than calling the criminals those that were not obeying the laws by the hegemonic authoritarian tyrannical megaforce, which shows its face through imperialism and colonialism (Nocella II, Seis, & Shantz 2019).

Black and Latinx bodies have always been a threat to White establishments. Hip Hop made for an easy target. Black critics of Hip Hop such as Shelby Steele, Jawanza Kunjufu, Niger Innis, and John McWhorter only added to the narrative of criminalization during the late 1980s through the mid-2000s. Critics such as these present a quandary of sorts; on the one end you have a critical voice of Black culture yet, on the other, they are Black and give credence to Bootstrap narratives and meritocracy ideologies which tend to support white structures and maintain white supremacy. Using shallow analysis and building on stereotypes, these types of detractors have only helped in providing fuel for the criminalization of Hip Hop culture. In other supernatural senses, Black pastors such as Dr. Calvin O. Butts III have help create a sense loss within the Hip Hop communicate within a very basic deduction of ill-advised research; in other words, if Ray-Ray was raised in the 'hood by a single mom, then he must listen to Hip Hop and rap music and be a thug. These types of worldviews, while simplistic and dangerous at best, are still present and remain center to policy makers in constructing laws. Another Black pastor, G. Craige Lewis, insists that all of Hip Hop culture is demonic and from a "Satanic realm." Again, this type of ideology continues to be in favor of a White Supremacist platform and one that ignores the critical and complex nature of Hip Hop. Moreover, in the current era we find ourselves in, aides in conspiratorial narratives that Hip Hop is part of the "illuminati" and controlled by other worldly forces—yes, these are current perceptions found easily on a Google search. To add, Blackness has been under attack at an even greater pace since the election of Barack Obama in 2008; the election of Donald Trump in 2016 only reinforced that notion even further. Thus, Hip Hop has been targeted and used as a means of punishment for Black and Latinx bodies. Saggin' pants policies, the prohibition of braided hair, loud music bans, baseball cap injunctions focused on Black and Latinx students, and even the use of the discourse of "Nigga" to discriminate against Black students are all part of this illegalization of Hip Hop.

Of course, this is not to say Hip Hop is not without critique and critical insight. But, it is important that the analysis and scholarship be centered around Hip Hop pedagogy (Parmar 2009; Nocella II, Parmar, & Stovall,

Introduction: Hip Hop History, Criminalization 5

2018; William 2010). In other words, one without knowledge, back-ground, and training would not haphazardly critique the field of sociology. So, it is true then of Hip Hop culture (Fernandes 2011).

This is one of the many reasons a book like this exists. Over the past two decades the scholarship surfacing in and throughout Hip Hop Studies has been grand—more than ever before. This is important and needed if we are ever to move out of the criminalization of Hip Hop culture. Further, true, accurate, and robust research continued to be needed within the culture. This was why the Journal Of Hip Hop Studies was established in 2012; to create a space for that scholarship and provide voice to an ever growing field of study. Hip Hop is interdisciplinary and can be used in many fields, not just the humanities and social sciences. Dr. Christopher Emdin has showed us, it can even be used to teach mathematics and other STEM areas! Thus, this book is to aid in the continued break down of negative tropes and stereotypes of and within Hip Hop culture. Let us turn now to the breakdown of the chapters.

Outline of the Book

In chapter one, "'No Homo': Hip-Hop, Homophobia, and Queer Justice," Hunt and Rhodes explore the intersection of hip hop studies and queer criminology, discussing the prominence of hypermasculinity and homophobia in hip hop. Through an exploratory study analyzing videos shared on the video blog WorldStarHipHop.com (WSHH), the authors examine and discuss various forms of violence directed at LGBTTQQIA+ people and how this is portrayed on the WSHH website. They conclude by discussing implications for the future of hip hop as well as queer and Hip Hop criminology.

In chapter two, "It's an Odd Future: Deviant Play and the Postmodern," Culton argues that Odd Future Collective's reframing of what can be considered authentic in hip hop is liberating for future artists and may help prevent future duplication of damaging stereotypes by hip hop artists. The genesis of Odd Future Collective is explored via an analysis of how public space is defined and the origins skateboarding, followed by a discussion of postmodernism and deviant play through the lens of Odd Future's work.

In chapter three, "Thug Life: Hip-Hop's Curious Relationship with Criminal Justice," Pond Cummings discusses how hip hop artists have expressed dissent for the criminal justice system since hip hop's inception, specifically speaking about how the system targets African American and Urban youth and attempts to use stigma and punitive punishment as means to prevent crime. The author then uses this lens to explore how hip hop has shaped the narrative around criminal justice in our Country, and how this will impact punishment and justice in the US moving forward.

In chapter four, "Música y Libertad," Mendoza writes from both personal and professional experience, exploring the origins and meaning of music itself, the evolution of hip hop culture, and the erasure of Latino culture from hip hop in its earlier days. This lays the context for a discussion of the field of Criminology today, why it is problematic, and how Hip Hop Criminology can lend a view that is more representative of those impacted by the current "justice" system.

In chapter five, "Stop and Search: Representations of Police Harassment in British Hip hop during the 1980s," Paor-Evans presents the evidence of police brutality and harassment— often cloaked behind the stop and search policy—through extensive lyrical, theoretical, and contextual analysis of hip hop songs in Britain, illustrating how these rap songs bring visibility to victims of structural racism.

In chapter six, "Legal Ambiguities and Cultural Power Struggles: The Moral and Legal Persecution of Rap in India," Gomes and Cardozo examine local Hip Hop music in India's influence on misogyny and rape culture through a criminological analysis, while juxtaposing this with discussion of how Hip Hop is scapegoated and that blaming Hip Hop does not address the root causes of misogyny and rape culture in India. Following is a discussion of the criminalization of this music and how the ambiguity of the laws creates opportunities for future prosecution of legitimate protest rappers in India using case studies from a variety of local artists.

Moving Forward

This book is not the be all and end all of Hip Hop criminology, but hopefully one of many efforts to develop a critical radical grassroots effort to dismantle classic orthodox criminology grounded in punishment, oppression, domination, retribution, and violence. This book and field is grounded in critical race theory, critical pedagogy (Freire 1997), social justice, intersectionality, Black liberation, youth justice, feminism, disability justice, LGBTTQQIA+ justice, immigration justice, decolonization, critical animal studies (Nocella II, Sorenson, Socha, & Matsuoka 2014), environmental justice, food justice, transformative justice, and healing justice (Daneshzadeh, Nocella II, Ward, and Washington 2022).

The origins of any historic thing are often dynamic and varied. In South Africa, the straightforward quest for peace and power-sharing by the indigenous peoples there was not so straight. Some were openly against peace, for

Introduction: Hip Hop History, Criminalization

opposing reasons, whether Nationalist whites or Indigenous freedom fighters, the struggle was in the veins of many. Others were for peace but did not agree on who else was truly for peace. Large numbers of indigenous peoples sided with reformed Nationalists to form coalitions that distrusted the majority indigenous ANC that led the struggle. Others simply trusted those like Nelson Mandela who had conducted themselves honorably and consistently from the beginning. Yet of that circumstance emerged the Truth and Reconciliation Council, former enemies shook hands and chatted, and a government by the people was born.

That was the 1990s, our era of Biggie and Pac, Wu, Bone Thugs N Harmony and Snoop. This was our TRUTH reconciled, the culmination of an almost diabolical street obsession with lyrical purity and relevance. And this too was dynamic. Verbal acrobatics had replaced literal ones— a changing of the Hip Hop guard where gangsters had things in their pockets that couldn't be turned upside down so they sought to flip your insides with agile cadences and gritty ad-libs.

Gone was the Good Foot, Salsa and neo-black Vaudeville; no longer could you see the Capoeristas of Brazil in the movements and swag of inner-city b-boys. Rather than causing angst they had become it. The censure of the past decade had created a dynamic synthesis, and it banged. It banged so hard that it brought truth to the idea that democracy had failed its underpinnings by denying equal access to the public sphere of non "normative" bodies.

Like all things original Hip Hop retained the dynamism of its nature. The public was coming to see virulently homophobic and even bigoted language not as a hate crime but as a dare. Hip Hop dared you to be different, to rep your difference, to be relevant in their arena or else. They were inclusive—inclusive of anyone who dared to find their voice in the midst of their marginalization, that forced recognition of themselves on a narcissistic and oblivious public. Arguably, it is the realization of this accepting, universally accessible culture that brought it into the mainstream and enshrined it as our Bonafede national visage. In this book you will navigate the vicissitudes of the conversation we have started here and journey through the national awakening to Hip Hop step by step as it occurs. Through the lens of Hunt and Rhodes we have all been gifted by this book with a glimpse at the genuine face of intersectionality and even queerness in America.

References

Alexander, M. (2012). *The new Jim Crow*. New Press.
Ball, J. A. (2011). *I mix what I like! A mixtape manifesto*. AK Press.

Boyd, T. (2004). *The new h.n.i.c.: The death of civil rights and the reign of hip hop.* New York University Press.

Chang, J. (2005). *Can't stop, won't stop: A history of the hip-hop generation.* St. Martin's Press.

Daneshzadeh, A., Nocella II, A. J., Ward, C., & Washington, A. R. (2022). *Fight the power: Breakin down hip hop activism.* Peter Lang Publishing.

Davis, A. (2003). *Are prisons obsolete?* Seven Stories Press.

Dyson, M. E. (2001). *Holler if you hear me: Searching for Tupac Shakur.* New York, NY: Basic Books.

Fernandes, S. (2011). *Close to the edge: The search of the global hip hop generation.* Verso.

Forman, M. (2007). Hip-Hop ya don't stop: Hip-hop history and historiography. In Forman, M. & Neal, M.A. (Eds.), That's The Joint!: The Hip-Hop Studies Reader (pp. 9-12). Routledge.

Freire, P. (1997). *Pedagogy of the oppressed.* Continuum.

Hodge, D. W. (2010). *The soul of hip hop: rims, timbs and a cultural theology.* IVP.

Hodge, D. W., Sawyer III, D. C., Nocella II, A. J., & Washington, A. R. (2020). *Hip-hop and dismantling the school-to-prison pipeline.* Peter Lang Publishing.

Nocella II, A. J., Parmar, P., & Stovall, D. (2018). *From education to incarceration: Dismantling the school to prison pipeline.* 2nd edition. Peter Lang Publishing.

Nocella II, A. J., Best, S., & McLaren, P. (2010). *Academic repression: Reflections from the academic industrial complex.* AK Press.

Nocella II, A. J., Sorenson, J., Socha, K., & Matsuoka, A. (2014). *Defining critical animal studies: An intersectional social justice approach for liberation.* Peter Lang Publishing.

Nocella II, A. J., Seis, M., & Shantz, J. (2019). Contemporary anarchist criminology: Against authoritarianism and punishment. Peter Lang Publishing.

Ogbar, J. O. G. (2007). *Hip-hop revolution: The culture and politics of rap.* University Press of Kansas.

Parmar, P. (2009). *Knowledge reigns supreme: The critical pedagogy of hip-hop artist KRS-ONE.* Sense Publishing.

Perry, I. (2004). *Prophets of the hood: Politics and poetics in hip hop.* Duke University Press.

Prier, D. D. (2012). *Culturally relevant teaching: Hip-Hop pedagogy in urban schools.* Peter Lang Publishing.

Rose, T. (1994). *Black noise: Rap music and black culture in contemporary America.* Wesleyan University Press.

Rose, T. (2008). *The hip hop wars: What we talk about when we talk about hip hop – and why it matters.* Basic Books.

William, L. (2010). "Hip-hop as a site of public pedagogy." In *Handbook of public pedagogy: Education and learning beyond schooling.* Eds. Jennifer A. Sandlin, Brian D. Schultz, and Jake Burdick. Routledge.

"No Homo": Hip-Hop, Homophobia, and Queer Justice

Andrea N. Hunt and Tammy D. Rhodes

Since its inception, hip hop has provided an alternative space for Black intellectualism (Jenkins, 2011; Belle, 2014) and served as a vehicle for social commentary and political activism. It has been a voice for the voiceless—a way for marginalized youth to have a sense of purpose and self-worth (Watkins, 2005). While there are positive images in hip hop around giving and earning respect (Kubrin, 2005; Smith, 2005) and friendship (Oware, 2011), hip hop has long been characterized as hyper-masculine and homophobic (Adams & Fuller 2006; Hill, 2009; Perry, 2004; Rose, 2008; Sharpley-Whiting, 2007). More recently, there has been an acknowledgment of LGBTQ rights within hip hop and an increase in artists who identify as LGBTQ (Taylor, 2018). Even with these changes, homophobia and transphobia remain within hip hop culture.

This chapter examines the relationship between queer justice and hip hop through an inductive content analysis of videos shared on the urban video blog, WorldStarHipHop.com (WSHH), along with a cursory exploration of viewer comments on each video within the sample. WSHH is a well-known brand associated with urban culture with online and social media platforms. They have a vast following with thousands of people visiting their site each day. They cater largely to young African American men and the violent fights on their site are often displayed alongside music videos of independent or up-and-coming hip hop artists. The fight videos become entertainment and the violence against LGBTQ people and LGBTQ people of color in particular is sensationalized and fetishized. The violence is glorified and thus the culture of violence is heightened for an already marginalized population. This research concludes by situating queer justice within hip hop and a call for hip hop to interrogate the role artists play in condoning violence against LGBTQ people.

Literature Review

Representation of LGBTQ People in Hip Hop

With the emergence of gangsta rap in the 1980s, the "badman" trope (Kelley, 1996) became the dominant portrayal of African American men in hip hop. With imagery and lyrics promoting hyper-masculinity and homophobia, corporate hip hop was openly hostile to queer identities during this time (Hill, 2009). This became essential in reifying an "authentic" Black masculinity that centered on struggle and growing up in ghettos around drugs and violence (Rodriquez, 2018). Rodriquez (2018) suggests that if struggle and oppression are the foundation of hip hop, then queer people of color are hip hop. However, corporate hip hop did not have a place for LGBTQ people with the exception of same-sex attractions between feminized women as fetishized objects of male conquest. Instead, Wilson (2007) describes the 1980s Black Gay Literary Movement as a counter-space for LGBTQ artists and later the underground hip hop scene that gave rise to artists such as Deep Dickollective (D/DC) who saw hip hop as a cultural and social space for the merging of identities.

Anti-gay rhetoric and threats of violence have been used in hip hop as a way to emasculate others and to police the boundaries of Black masculinity. For example, lyrics with homophobic slurs and accusations about an artist's sexual identity (namely male artists who tend to have more at stake) are a way exert power and to discredit them. Hill (2009) refers to this as lyrical outing and traces this back to 1989 with the rumors of Big Daddy Kane having HIV. At the time, HIV was associated with gay men and this led people to question Kane's sexuality. Hill (2009) notes that Kane denounced these rumors in 1993 in true hip hop fashion by rapping about it on the track "Give it to Me" and even went to other measures to assure his heterosexuality and masculinity (e.g., posing partially nude in *Playgirl*).

The use of "no homo" has become a disclaimer in rap to counteract any misconceptions in lyrics and serves as a form of linguistic self-defense. It is a way to distance oneself from accusations around sexuality and a way to have homosocial bonds with other men (Brown, 2011; Oware, 2011). Oware (2011) illustrates this by suggesting that you can love another man "no homo" and show it as long as you are still portraying yourself in a hyper-masculine way by objectifying women. This is accomplished through heterosexual sex-talk and even through shared homoerotic sexual conquests such as "running trains" on women or group sex (as expressed in Snoop Dogg's "Ain't No Fun (If the Homies Can't Have None)") (Hill, 2009). Rodriquez (2018) suggests that the real issue is being seen as effeminate, that more hate exists towards the effeminate (i.e., femiphobia [Dyson, 2006]), and that you can be gay as long as you are masculine and tough.

The recent embrace of a more runway style or queer-embraced fashion style threatens the hyper-masculine mainstream identity of hip hop (Penny, 2012). This style is associated with a metrosexual image and it represents close proximity to the cultural elite who are often upper class gay men in fashion (Hill, 2009; Penny, 2012). Taylor (2018) also suggests that the increasing representation of LGBTQ artists has shifted the conversation in hip hop and held hip hop more accountable. This has led artists who used the term faggot or gay in the past to defend their usage or to recant it. Kehrer (2018) questions whether hip hop artists are more accepting or whether it is the need for corporate hip hop to adapt to larger cultural influences. Either way, audiences are still more likely to embrace artists that are allies rather than LGBTQ artists which continues to keep LBTGQ artists on the margins of hip hop.

New (and Emerging) Media, Aggression, and Violence

New and emerging media is often contrasted to old media that was more print or television based. The term "new media" has been used for decades and refers to internet or computer-based technologies with emerging media indicating more interactive digital technologies, faster speed of information delivery, and the increasing use of algorithms to personalize media experiences. New and emerging media have more user-generated content than old media and have the capacity to be shared and consumed globally. Hitchens (2019) argues that new forms of media have the capacity to shape ideas around marginalized identities, either through the maintenance of racism, sexism, or homophobia and/or by providing counter-narratives that do not perpetuate systems of inequality.

Previous research has focused on user-generated content (i.e., fight/violent videos) on social media as a way to gain status or becoming social media famous (Hitchens, 2019; Eschmann & Butler, 2013; Rhodes & Hunt, 2018). These online fight videos are a form of exploitation and fetishization of violence where violence against marginalized groups in particular is a form of entertainment that goes viral. Previous research in this area has primarily focused on girl fights among teens (Hitchens, 2019; Larkin & Dwyer, 2016; Rhodes & Hunt, 2018). While this research provides valuable insight into the gendered elements of online violence, it does not explicitly focus on the experiences of LGBTQ people of color.

WorldStarHipHop.com

Taylor (2018) argues that by focusing on lyrics alone hides the fact that the larger industry (including new media e.g., WSHH) is a part of creating a structure that pushes LGBTQ people out of hip hop. WWSH was founded in 2005 by Lee "Q" O'Denat. According to the description of WSHH on their Facebook page (2019), "WorldStarHipHop.com is the premiere online hip hop destination. Artists and brands alike have utilized the platform that [sic] WorldStarHipHop.com to debut their music videos, singles, apparel, and products given the sites traffic and loyal audience." WSHH advertises itself on Facebook as the voice of hip hop with the "latest headlines and hottest content in urban media" (2009) and has active content on Facebook, Instagram, YouTube, Twitter, Snapchat, and the website. They have 9.6 million followers on Facebook, 2.2 million followers on Instagram, and 4.5 million followers on Twitter.

While the site originally started as a space for people to download music from minor labels and independent artists, the scope quickly expanded to include amateur fight/violent videos (Cramer, 2016). This originally started around 2011 with a group of teens yelling "WorldStar" while beating security guard Daniel Endara (Jacobson, 2012). Endara's beating was filmed and later went viral. The subsequent yelling of "WorldStar" in other fight videos helped ensure that these uncensored videos would be posted to the site. Once these videos go viral, the fighters, videographers, and bystanders can gain attention and symbolic capital in an attempt to become micro-celebrities (Hitchens, 2019) or the "new famous" (Rhodes & Hunt, 2018). Cramer (2016) suggests that the violent videos on WSHH also create a digital proximity to the subject where Hitchens (2019) says that Black misery is constructed as both humorous and despicable. These videos perpetuate the idea of urban violence with WSHH creating the narrative that there is not a place for LGBTQ people of color in urban communities or in hip hop. WSHH is careful to not only be seen as a user-generated content space for fight vides by also focusing on music videos. In doing so, WSHH is making it clear that it is still hip hop.

Theoretical Framework

Queer criminology has expanded in the last decade with the help of practitioners and scholars such Mogul, Ritchie, and Whitlock (2011) and Buist and

Lenning (2016) who have helped conceptualize this subfield of criminology. Queer criminology counters the notion that queers identities are deviant and argues that LGBTQ people have been marginalized in the field of criminology (Ball et al., 2019; Russell, 2016; Module et al., 2011). Queer criminology draws attention to LGBTQ people as victims and offenders by focusing on experiences of harassment, discrimination, and violence. Past research has examined intra-familial and interpersonal violence and how LGBTQ people navigate their safety after violence (Ball et al., 2019; Panfil, 2018). Queer criminology is not grounded in a reductionist view of LGBTQ experiences but rather is keenly aware that racism, sexism, and social class inequality shapes interpersonal and institutional violence. This is especially true for the transgender women of color who have an even higher rate of victimization compared to other LGBTQ people (Buist & Lenning, 2016; Panil, 2018). Even as criminological research has adopted a more intersectional and queer criminology lens, we still lack an adequate understanding of the social media and online phenomenon of fight/violent videos with LGBTQ people as the center of this violence. The current research aims to extend this line of research by using queer criminology to explore the nature of violence against LGBTQ people in videos posted to WSHH.

Methodology

This research is guided by queer criminology as a broad theoretical and practical approach to move LGBTQ people from the margins to the center of criminological research (Buist & Lenning, 2016). This is an exploratory study using an inductive content analysis to examine how aggression, violence, and bullying of LGBTQ people of color is portrayed on WorldStarHipHip.com. There were 33 videos selected for analysis using "gay", "lesbian", and "transgender" as the search terms on the WSHH website. Each video selected for the analysis was uploaded to the WSHH website in 2019–2020 and had views ranging from 127,000 to 1,325,800. The videos varied in length from 13 seconds to one hour and included original videos and interviews of African American celebrities. A preliminary analysis was conducted using a half of the videos to develop the initial themes followed by a full analysis of the 33 videos. The videos were coded independently by both researchers and the findings were compared. The coding of the videos were consistent between both researchers resulting in 100% inter-rater reliability with both researchers identifying additional details in the videos that were important to the analysis. The three primary themes are not mutually exclusive and some videos showed a combination of two of the three themes. The themes are presented in Table 1 along with the number of videos in which the theme was identified.

Table 1. Themes in LGBTQ videos from WorldStarHipHop.com used in the analysis

Theme	Number of videos
Giving you life, and you can't handle it.	12/33
Petty Level 100!	19/33
When a read becomes revenge	24/33

Findings

It is important to first provide some context for the videos. When submitting videos to WSHH, users agree that they have the necessary rights in the video to authorize WSHH the use and reuse of the audio and visual material in the video. In reality, this is not always the case and WSHH has been sued several times by artists and others whose images were used on WSHH (Digital Media Law Project, 2012; Newswire, 2016; Vibe, 2009). The videos in this sample appear to be submitted by someone who was either an onlooker, someone directly involved in the situation capturing the encounters, or someone recording interviews with celebrities on podcasts, The Breakfast Club, or other media outlets. After watching half of the videos, patterns began to emerge that were then documented to create the themes that were used for the analysis. The themes that emerged were "Giving you life, and you can't handle it", "Petty Level 100!", and "When a read becomes revenge". Regarding the videos that showed more violence, eight of those took place outside with bystanders witnessing victimization. The bystanders were usually people of similar demographics to the perpetrators. Only two of the videos seemed to take place in residential locations. None of the videos showed children or adolescents, which was intentional because the search did not include juveniles.

Giving You Life and You Can't Handle It

To maintain the credibility as a hip hop blog, WSHH showcases videos of artist and celebrities and reinforces society's interest in their lifestyles. Along with their fashion, cars, and relationships, the extreme fascination with the sexuality of celebrities becomes obsessive. No one is off limits of being accused of "dabbling" in a down-low lifestyle. Such is the case with the theme, "Giving you life, and you can't handle it." While fans idolize artists and celebrities,

"No Homo": Hip-Hop, Homophobia, and Queer Justice

they are also quick to buy into the drama surrounding their sexuality. Some celebrities are open about their sexuality (e.g., Lil Nas X), which does not mean that they are not still scrutinized while others may also be under the microscope regarding accusations about who they are and how they love. For example, WSHH had top hits on videos including Young Thug and Malik Yoba. Rapper Young Thug is known to express himself through his clothing. While he has explained multiple times that he is not gay, many of his fans have accused of him being gay because he wears "feminine" clothing, citing the cover of his album, *Jeffery*, where he wears a dress. Young Thug's persona and clothing is more consistent with a queer-embraced fashion style that is emerging in hip hop which Penny (2012) suggests threatens the mainstream identity of hip hop that has been so entrenched in masculine tropes.

In 2019, Malik Yoba gave an interview in which he expressed that he did not differentiate between women and transwomen and found himself to be attracted to both. This was in a response to backlash from an Instagram post that he wrote expressing that people should love whom they want to love. For many, they immediately saw him as "gay". He then did several interviews, some posted on WSHH, where he explained his position about love and transwomen. R&B artist, Tank, did two interviews (the videos were posted on WSHH) where he explained that partaking in sexual acts with a man did not make him gay. His fans and others disagreed as seen in the comment sections on WSHH.

Most celebrities are willing to position certain aspects of their lives publicly, but seem to push back against their fans if they push too far into the lives of their children. Though some believe that their children are off limits, newly retired athlete, Dwayne Wade, whose daughter Zaya recently came out as a transgender girl, proved that even children of celebrities are scrutinized. In one of the videos in the sample, Wade talked openly about conversations that he had with his family prior to Zaya announcing that she was transgender. He feared that she would face backlash, but that he would always protect her and keep her safe. The comment section under this video on WSHH was mixed with some people supporting Wade while others vehemently condemned Dwayne, his wife, actress Gabrielle Union, and Zaya. Retired athlete and businessman, Magic Johnson, whose son EJ is openly gay, has also had to deal with public backlash. Witnessing the difference in public backlash has been astonishing in that people have expressed that Zaya is too young to know if she is a "girl or not". Zaya is 13 while EJ was 22 when he came out.

Petty Level 100!

One of the urban terms for a person who is creating drama or "mess" is to label them as "petty". Many of the videos show perpetuators who purposely misgender or mislabel LGBTQ people as a form of intimidation and verbal violence. Even in the interviews or videos where celebrities are the focus, extreme cursing and pettiness is used in the conversation. In a video where rapper Tekashi 69 was discussed on a podcast, he was called a "bitch" and the commentator compared his snitching to performing a gay act. Calling him a "bitch" was to demean him by making him appear weak and further decreasing his street credibility. In other videos in the sample, using terms such as "faggot" was a way for the perpetrators to draw attention to effeminate Black (i.e., femiphobia [Dyson, 2006]), men in attempts to emasculate them. The word "faggot", just by being spoken, operates in two ways. It hurts the victim while also creating "clout" for the perpetrator. For example, in a video where a woman continued to "out" her ex-partner by accusing him of having an affair with another man, she continued to demean him by calling him a "faggot". Even when he begged her to stop, she continued to call him a "faggot" and he clearly became emotional. It was as if it hurt him more to be called a "faggot" than the actual "outing" itself.

In the videos that consisted of misgendering transwomen, the victims were called names that indicated their sex assigned at birth or purposely referred to using the wrong pronouns. This was often accompanied by extreme cursing. By doing this, the perpetrators were seeking to emotionally and mentally victimize by invoking a response that either turned to anger or shared violence. In this analysis, this often happened in public settings when transwomen of color were shopping (e.g., shoe store, car rental, McDonald's), in other group settings (e.g., nightclubs), or online where more masculine Black gay men were using these tactics as a form of verbal dominance.

When a Read becomes Revenge

Violence has always been used as a way to police masculinity among minoritized groups (Mogul et al., 2011). In such cases, Black and Latinx LGBTQ people become easy targets for vitriol and violence. In the urban community, a "read" can be a snarky disagreement. However, when that disagreement turns into violence (whether verbal or physical), it becomes revenge for that "read". Several videos showed people arguing, yelling, and threatening the physical safety of another person in the video. This was often an escalation of the pettiness illustrated in the previous section. During one of Malik Yoba's interviews, he became so visibly upset, cursed at the interviewer, and stormed out of the room. His reaction was in defense of the questions asked about previous allegations of sex with an underage transwoman, but also to show the interviewer that he could not challenge his masculinity and get away with it.

While some of these videos show verbal intimidation and violence, others focus more on physical violence. For example, in one video a shorter, gay, Latinx man slapped and punched his partner (assuming they are partners), who is a transwoman. In examining the video, she initiated the argument or read but did not defend herself when it turned to violence. In another video, a group of Black men are standing in an apartment. The victim is standing in the middle explaining to his friends that he is gay. His friends all gang up on him and beat him down to the floor. In another video, a transwoman is cursing at a man and he begins to beat her up. Another man jumps in and begins to beat on her as well. By the end of the video, she gains her footing and fights back, eventually winning the fight, but not without taking tremendous blows to the face and head. In another video, a transwoman is tazed several times in a public setting with onlookers watching. One of the most unconscionable things to process are the comments under these videos. The commenters are given access to write their thoughts as reactions to any of the videos on WSHH without being censored. Most of the comments under these videos are violent in nature, in which they insinuate and co-sign verbal, emotional, and physical violence against LGBTQ people.

Discussion and Conclusion

Queer criminology aims to reduce the invisibility of LGBTQ violence, and in doing so, to move the experiences of LGBTQ people out of the margins of criminological research. While this subfield of criminology is growing, we still lack an adequate understanding of the social media and online phenomenon of fight/violent videos with LGBTQ people as the center of this violence. The paradox here is that the posting of videos of LGBTQ people on WSHH makes them more visible, but the violence against them is seen as entertainment (keeping them still invisible). Using an inductive content analysis of data gathered from videos on WSHH, we argue that WSHH shapes larger narratives around LGBTQ people and contributes to the glorification of violence against LGBTQ people of color. We summarize the findings below and discuss the implications for the future of hip hop.

Our inductive content analysis showed perpetrators performed some form of violence (verbal, emotional, physical) in 28 out of 33 videos. This means that 28 videos showed some type of behavior where perpetrators participated in misabeling/misgendering folx, cursing in celebrity videos, and cursing/ fighting in videos. Selnow (1985) explains that this constant use of profanity, especially by men, is not only a form of emotional violence, but also a way to exert dominance, which earns street credibility in more urban communities. In the hip hop community, not speaking out against videos like these essentially condones this behavior. While the violent videos against the LGBTQ community may be seen as entertainment, they can also be categorized as fetishization or violent obsession (Chen, 2018). Comments are also posted underneath the videos that could be easily categorized as internet bullying. Abreu and Kenny (2018) found that significant internet bullying of LGBTQ people is a predictor of health issues, specifically mental health, in LGBTQ youth of color. The comments under these videos not only call for violence against the people in the videos but for continuous violence of LGBTQ people in general.

This research also shows that potential for the integration of hip hop studies and queer criminology. Panfil (2018) argues for work that makes meaningful contributions regarding the experiences of LGBTQ people, which may not appear in current criminological research. For example, research in hip hop has expounded on this. Panfil (2018) suggests that queer criminology's potential lies in its ability to address timely questions in an increasingly diverse world using a multidisciplinary focus. Likewise, hip hop studies offers the same potential and has responded to this call for over a decade (see Hill, 2009; Wilson, 2007).

Hip hop in general has been reluctant to move LGBTQ artists and experiences from the margins. However, Penny (2012) and Taylor (2018) both suggest a shift in hip hop towards more acceptance but this has been met with some criticism. As Watkins (2005, p. 256) so eloquently stated,

> The purists in the movement believe that in the midst of a commercial explosion hip hop has lost its edge, its spirit of innovation, and its capacity for inspiration. But this view assumes that hip hop has only one destiny, only one true historic course. As the voices, people, and places that define hip hop grow more diverse, the movement continues to develop many different identities and interests. Despite a fascinating history and undeniable influence in America's pop cultural, political, and intellectual life, the struggle for hip hop, amazingly, has only just begun.

Our hope is that this research situates queer justice within hip hop and creates a call for hip hop artists and fans alike to examine the role they play in condoning violence against LGBTQ people. Hip hop has given so many artists and fans a place to find themselves and negotiate their identities, and it is time that LGBTQ artists and fans had the same opportunity.

References

Abreu, R. L., & Kenny, M. C. (2018). Cyberbullying and LGBTQ youth: A systematic literature review and recommendations for prevention and intervention. *Journal of Childhood Adolescent Trauma, 11,* 81–97.

Adams, T., & Fuller, D. (2006). The words have changed but the ideology remains the same: Misogynistic lyrics in rap music. *Journal of Black Studies, 36,* 938–957.

Ball, M., Broderick, T., Ellis, J., Dwyerd, A., & Asquith, N. L. (2019). Introduction: Queer(y)ing justice. *Current Issues in Criminal Justice, 31*(3), 305–310. https://doi.org/10.1080/10345329.2019.1643058

Belle, C. (2014). From Jay-Z to Dead Prez: Examining representations of black masculinity in mainstream versus underground hip-hop music. *Journal of Black Studies, 45*(4), 287–300.

Brown, J. R. (2011). No homo. *Journal of Homosexuality, 58,* 299–314. doi: 10.1080/00918369.2011.546721

Buist, C. L., & Lenning, E. (2016). *Queer criminology: New directions in critical criminology.* Routledge.

Chen, Y. A. (2018). Media coverage and social changes: Examining valence of portrayal of the LGBT community from 2000 to 2014 in two U.S. magazines. *Intercultural Communication Studies, 27*(1), 83–96.

Cramer, L. M. (2016). Race at the interface: Rendering Blackness on WorldStarHipHop.com. *Film Criticism, 40*(2). http://dx.doi.org/10.3998/fc.13761232.0040.205

Digital Media Law Project. (2012, July 17). *Scott v. WorldStarHipHop, Inc.* http://www.dmlp.org/threats/scott-v-worldstarhiphop-inc

Dyson, M. E. (2006). *Holler if you hear me: Searching for Tupac Shakur.* Basic Civitas Books.

Hill, M. (2009). Scared straight: Hip-hop, outing, and the pedagogy of queerness. *The Review of Education, Pedagogy, and Cultural Studies, 31,* 29–54.

Hitchens, B. K. (2019). Girl fights and the online media construction of Black female violence and sexuality. *Feminist Criminology, 14*(2), 173–197. doi: 10.1177/1557085117723705

Jacobson, M. (2012). WorldStar, baby! *New York Magazine.* https://nymag.com/news/features/worldstar

Kehrer, L. (2018). A love song for all of us?: Macklemore's "Same Love" and the myth of Black homophobia. *Journal of the Society for American Music, 12*(4), 425–448. doi:10.1017/S1752196318000354

Kubrin, C. (2005). Gangstas, thugs, and hustlas: Identity and the code of the street in rap music. *Social Problems, 52,* 360–378.

Jenkins, T. (2011). A beautiful mind: Black male intellectual identity and hip-hop culture. *Journal of Black Studies, 42,* 1231–1251.

Larkin, A., & Dwyer, A. (2016). Fighting like a girl ... or a boy? An analysis of videos of violence between young girls posted on online fight websites. *Current Issues in Criminal Justice, 27*, 269–284. https://doi.org/10.1080/10345329.2016.12036046

Mogul, J. L., Ritchie, A. J., & Whitlock, K. (2011). *Queer (in)justice: The criminalization of LGBT people in the United States*. Beacon Press.

Newswire. (2016, July 20). *World Star Hip Hop gossip blog sued by rapper Khaotic for posting leaked sex tape says artist's attorney Richard Wolfe*. https://www.newswire.com/news/world-star-hip-hop-gossip-blog-sued-by-rapper-khaotic-for-posting-5039640

Oware, M. (2011). Brotherly love: Homosociality and Black masculinity in gangsta rap music. *Journal of African American Studies, 15*, 22–39.

Panfil, V. R. (2018). Young and unafraid: Queer criminology's unbounded potential. *Palgrave Communications, 4*(110). https://doi.org/10.1057/s41599-018-0165-x

Patton, D. U., Eschmann, R. D., & Butler, D. A. (2013). Internet banging: New trends in social media, gang violence, masculinity and hip hop. *Computers in Human Behavior, 29*, A54–A59. https://doi.org/10.1016/j.chb.2012.12.035

Penny, J. (2012). "We don't wear tight clothes": Gay panic and queer style in contemporary hip hop. *Popular Music and Society, 35*(3), 321–332. https:doi.org/10.1080/03007766.2011.578517

Perry, I. (2004). *Prophets of the hood: Politics and poetics in hip hop*. Durham: Duke University Press.

Rhodes, T. D., & Hunt, A. N. (2018). The new famous: Deconstructing social media girl-fights. In K. McQueeney & A. Malone (Eds.), *Girls, aggression, and intersectionality: Transforming the discourse of "mean girls" in the United States* (pp. 90–105). Routledge.

Rodriquez, N. S. (2018). Hip-hop's authentic masculinity: A quare reading of Fox's Empire. *Television & New Media, 19*(3), 225–240. doi: 10.1177/1527476417704704

Rose, T. (2008). *The hip hop wars: What we talk about when we talk about hip hop—And why it matters*. New York: Basic Civitas Books.

Russell, E. K. (2017). Queer penalties: The criminal justice paradigm in lesbian and gay anti-violence politics. *Critical Criminology, 25*, 21–35. doi: 10.1007/s10612-016-9337-4

Selnow, G. W. (1985). Sex differences in uses and perceptions of profanity. *Sex Roles, 12*, 303–310.

Sharpley-Whiting, T. (2007). *Pimp's up, ho's down*. New York: New York University Press.

Smith, S. L. (2005). From Dr. Dre to dismissed: Assessing violence, sex, and substance use on MTV. *Critical Studies in Media Communication, 22*, 89–98.

Taylor, B. (2018). Homophobia in hip hop. In T. Riggs (Ed.), *St. James encyclopedia of hip hop culture* (pp. 211–215). St. James Press.

Vibe. (2009, November 12). *50 Cent files infringement lawsuit against Worldstarhiphop*. https://www.vibe.com/2009/11/50-cent-files-infringement-lawsuit-against-worldstarhiphop

Wilson, M. (2007). Post-pomo hip hop homos: Hip-hop art, gay rappers, and social change. *Social Justice, 34*(1), 117–140.

WorldStar Hip Hop. (2019). *About* [Facebook page]. Facebook. Retrieved March 30, 2020 from https://www.facebook.com/pg/worldstarhiphop/about/

It's an Odd Future: Deviant Play and the Postmodern

Kenneth R. Culton

The postmodern hip-hop collective Odd Future, led by Tyler the Creator and consisting primarily of members Hodgy Beats, Left Brain, Domo Genesis, Earl Sweatshirt, Mike G, Frank Ocean, Syd the Kid, Jasper Dolphin and Taco Bennet has spearheaded what some have called the rise of alternative hip-hop. Originating in 2008, Odd Future has diffused into numerous solo projects, most notably the work of Tyler the Creator, whose album IGOR won the Grammy for best rap album in 2020. Tyler's work goes beyond hip-hop as he has built a successful career that now includes clothing design, comedy writing, show promoting, and most recently acting. I will consider the origins of the collective first, that primarily being the streets and skateparks where they met and shared their creative energy. Next, I'll look in more detail at how Odd Future earns the label of a postmodern collective by their reframing of what can be considered authentic in hip-hop. This, I will argue, is ultimately liberating for themselves and future artists who, while working within industry norms, have typically been compelled to reproduce damaging stereotypes.

The youth subcultural terrain that spawned hip-hop and just about any other subculture is a marginalized space. It is best to begin the investigation of Odd Future and other such postmodern collectives as groups arising from activity that is marginalized (such as skateboarding as we will see), and occurring in the subcultural milieu. As such the actions of members are deemed deviant due to their social location or place in an ongoing struggle. Stephen Pfohl (1994) explains how perception of actions, ideas, and ways of being that we consider either normal and good, or deviant and law breaking, are merely the outcome of this struggle or "battle." He writes:

> "The story of deviance and social control is a battle story. It is a story of the battle to control ways people think, fell, and behave. It is a story of winners and losers and the strategies people us in struggles with one another. Winners in the battle to control 'deviant acts' are crowned with the halo of goodness, acceptability, normality. Losers are viewed as living outside the boundaries of social life as it ought to be, outside the 'common sense' of society itself (Pfohl 1994: 2)."

Such battles are sometimes explicit, as in the fight for marijuana legalization, where the winning side is able to situate their position firmly within the safe confines of propriety. Other struggles are not so public or well reported, such as those of the homeless to find legitimacy, including often merely the right to exist without enduring stigma. Once the winner as crowned and loser so labeled next we find that institutions, especially that of criminal justice, are more than willing to codify what were once arbitrary differences into concrete practice.

Richard Quinney (1975) explains that when individuals are acted against criminality arises. It is those higher on the class ladder that are most effectively able to apply deviant labels, while the lower classes are denied a seat at the table where judgments are meted out. Quinney lays out a critical conflict-based way to understand how our very notions of what is normal versus what we consider to be deviant are constructed. The dominant class is the one who both develops notions of deviant behavior and applies those definitions in practice through the legal apparatus (Quinney, 1975). Jeffrey Reiman and Paul Leighton, in the classic work *The Rich Get Richer and the Poor Get Prison*, (2010) add that "it is no surprise that legislators and judges—those who makes the laws that define criminality and those who interpret those laws—are predominantly members of the upper classes (Reiman & Leighton, 2010: 188–9)." The target of the system of criminal justice is most often young, poor, urban, and (disproportionally) black (Reiman & Leighton, 2010).

Just as there are behaviors and ways of being that are undermined by those who get to make such decisions, space itself is often subject to the same process. Henri Lefabvre articulates this in his book *The Production of Space* (1991), a Marxian analysis of how space is organized. For Lefabvre space is organized by human beings with human interests in mind. But the primary spatial arrangement today is what he calls *abstract space*, or space dominated by capitalists with capitalistic goals being paramount. The *solution* for abstract space for Lefabvre is *differential space* or space that is liberated from the control of capitalists. Such differential spaces are uncommon today as our landscape is increasingly dominated by shopping-malls, corporate coffee shops, and office buildings. When the public square is no longer public reclaiming, or better yet repurposing space is an important and potentially defiant act. Skateboarding is such a practice, occurring, from its subcultural roots, in abstract space and becoming an exhibit for how we may reclaim corporate space for the purpose of pleasure and the joy of unfettered creativity.

Next, I briefly consider the history of the skateboarding subculture and the potential role of the subculture as a contributing social force catalyzing the creative zeal of the postmodern hip-hop collective Odd Future.

Skateboarding: The Origin of an Ethos

Skateboarding as it is known today originated in 1970s Santa Monica, California in the vicinity of the remnants of Pacific Ocean Park, an abandoned and decaying amusement park. A group of young misfits from the gritty Venice neighborhood made a pastime of surfing and skateboarding. These Z-boys of "Dogtown" would, with the aid of a chronicle in *Skateboarder* magazine, become legendary. Inspired by father figure Jeff Ho the Zepher skate team, including members Tony Alva, Jay Adams and others, pioneered an irreverent skate style that was unlike anything other skaters were doing. Mainstream skateboarding in the 1970s was an innocent leisure activity where practitioners held no particular outsider status. The Z-boys changed all that. Kids from broken homes on the wrong side of the tracks brought a brashness to skateboarding. For them it was a way of life, not a leisure activity. In the pursuit of greater challenges and greater thrills the Z-boys would eventually move beyond conquering streets and other slabs of concrete to actually break into the backyards of wealthy Californians to transform their swimming pools into skate ramps. Half-pipe skating as it is known today, now an Olympic event, originated from the dogged tenacity of these SoCal lads dubbed "urban guerrillas" by Craig Stecyk, who took risks, and broke norms for the love of skateboarding (Beato, 2007).

Writing of skateboarding's development in the 1980s Robert Rundquist in "Street Skateboarding and the Government Stamp of Approval" recounts the following from Donald Bell in the skateboarding magazine *Heckler*:

> "Street Skaters use the surrounding concrete covered modern landscape as a canvas for personal artistic expression. The art of street skating lies in its ability to incorporate objects of architectural utility (curbs, benches, driveways, handrails) into a high speed dance that critiques the significance of the object and shows to those with open minds the beauty that can be found in the everyday...I spent my youth destroying people's confidence in the absolute meaning of these objects... (Rundquist, 2007: 183–4)."

Skateboarders go where they shouldn't, and they do things that were unintended. They subvert utilitarian design as they transform serious features of the environment into props for their playful amusement. In doing so they take on risks and as such the activity can be seen as a response to the predictability and boredom of everyday life (Haenfler 2014: 38). In discussing Lyng's (1990) concept of *edgework*, Haenfler goes on to write:

> "Institutions increasingly regulate, monitor, even constrain our lives, resulting in alienation and a feeling of lacking control over one's life. Some people crave the freedom and sense of control found in the exploring the boundaries between order and disorder, normality and deviance." (Haenfler, 2014: 38)"

It is notable that skateboarding has been a predominantly white, male, middle-class subculture, and only recently have black youths, mostly suburban and middle-class themselves, begun to have a presence in the subculture. It is not surprising that boredom with the supposed idyllic suburban landscape elicits unrest among white kids and black kids alike. Perhaps it could be perceived as an achievement that some black and brown kids have advanced enough in socio-economic status to now live in environments where they can be bored senseless in whitewashed suburbia rather than traumatized by the violence and chaos of urban America. Before moving on to better grasp the impact of skateboarding on Odd Future's postmodern creative output it will be valuable to consider the theoretical underpinnings of the subculture concept and how participating in a subculture like skateboarding can alter life trajectories of participants.

Tyler the Creator was detained in 2011 for skating past a police officer, disturbing the peace, and loitering. The charges can be deciphered to read Tyler as a human who made the error of existing in abstract space in a way that threatened the typical expectations of those who decide how people should move through it, i.e., *hegemonic* space (*See* Gramsci, 1971). Of course, it would be unreasonable to assume that there was no provocation on Tyler's part, in fact, the impetus to provoke is very much a key characteristic of he and his groups creative career.

> By the way, I got sixty fuckin' Wolves that'll guard me
> They skate hard brash black hoodies, try somethin'
> Make sure your fuckin' feeling end up up in a glad bag
> Fuck all your opinions, I'm tie 'em up in a shoestring
> And fuck the fat lady, it's over when all the kids sing
> (Okonma, 2011)

To be a part of a subculture is to dwell in the margins. By not being *normal* and refusing to do *normal* things the subculturalist will be labeled deviant by society. Or seen another way, normalcy is achieved by labeling the other as an outsider (Becker 1963). When applied, the deviant label is hard to shake and as such subculturalists often internalize the sense of themselves as outsiders. Their labelers, or "mainstream," come to be seen as the opposition. As the subculturalist descends, or ascends as it may be, into greater involvement in the subculture they are more likely to internalize the values and norms of the deviant group. The process tends to become a feedback loop of sorts as the subcultural participant grows more distant from mainstream culture as she or he submits a greater and greater investment in the alternative. For many subculturalists the label outsider was given prior to subcultural involvement. The feeling of being an outsider then would be the common thread for those, like the Z-boys of Dogtown, who were denied the approval of mainstream society. Tyler the Creator explained that he went to a different school every year growing up. His primary interests were music and skating. And it was at the skate park where he would meet future members of Odd Future. Perhaps their shared identification with the skateboarding subculture as well as a sense of otherness common among subculturalists led to the communalism and comradery that would shape all of their future endeavors.

Hip-Hop as a Postmodern Subculture

"I would put hip-hop forward as one form of radical postmodernism, a postmodernism whose representational strategies, while complex and contradictory, do not for that reason lose their liberatory potential." (Potter, 1995: 9)

Afrika Bambaataa outlined hip-hop culture as containing four basic elements, Dj-ing, MC-ing, breakdancing, and graffiti. As hip-hop expands and diversifies we can begin to include such practices as skateboarding. Tyler the Creator embodies this and playfully turns his attention to the elitist practice of golf as well. He turns "wolf gang" into "golf wang" in some songs and much of his clothing line is adorned with the word GOLF. In a 2014 interview with Larry King Tyler explains that he just likes the word golf and how it looks. But perhaps there is an unconscious effort to invade spaces such as the golf course, and in doing so undermine the privileged position and perceived sense of purity they hold as exclusive spaces reserved for the dominant order. In fact, the whole of the subcultural project can be seen as undermining the privileged dominant position by presenting to all what Genesis P. Orridge called "alternate ways of being."

M.K. Assante, Jr. (2008) takes issue with Baudrillardian simulations such as the media's depiction of the ghetto that hip-hop artists tend to consciously or unconsciously reproduce for the amusement of white suburban youth who are the greatest consumers of the music. The *reel* as it is referred to by Assante is a poor copy of the *real*, or essential truths of black culture. In response we should see the emancipatory potential in in a new hip-hop generation that embraces the *real*. The text presented here in the form of artifacts primarily put forth by the Odd Future collective does not represent such a narrative, one that is linear moving from a place of disadvantage to one of empowerment. Indeed, some hip-hop artists and their work could be described in this way, as a path to greater enlightenment. But, simply put, the artists presented here are on a path of deconstruction, which one might quite accurately note, is no path at all. They dwell in what philosopher Dennis Smith calls the postmodern habitat where "the sense of ambivalence becomes dominant" and the postmodern perspective becomes a *"productive force* that shapes how individuals construct their lives. (Smith, 2013: 154)." In fact, we will see that much of the work produced here can be identified through its ambivalence, where opposing positions coexist and rise to surface often without warning. In this creative landscape morality itself is brought into question, along with notions of good or bad. That said, the postmodern artist is no nihilist, there is a will to *say* something, as well as a notion that what is being said is of value, even if the statement is merely, "I detest your rules." As well will see while delving into the work of the Odd Future collective, this is present, and quite a bit more.

What They Do

> Fuck your traditions, fuck your positions
> Fuck your religion, fuck your decisions
> See they're not mine so you gotta let 'em go
> (Okonma, 2011)

Postmodernism can be conceived of in many ways, but a common application regarding arts and culture is to see it as a reaction to, and ultimate rejection of, modernist traditions and perceived "elitism" (Hooper 2012), likewise an effort to "blur the distinction between pop culture and high art (Molokov & Zueva, 2017: 1359)." Before moving on it is important to briefly introduce some notions commonly utilized by postmodern thinkers. I will then present some of the work of these artists as categorized samples that will be given greater meaning, or at least to whatever extent this can be said in a postmodern context.

First, imploding. This is the tendency for phenomena in the postmodern world to explode in on itself thereby destroying the phenomena and previous perceptions of it (Baudrillard, 1983). Imploding reality is to accelerate the reduction of meaning through the strategic application of absurdity. This is most visible through boundary defying play, a most common act among the OF collective.

Second, narratives and deconstruction. From a postmodern perspective, meta-narratives or stories about stories are suspect because they claim objective truth (*See* Lyotard, 1985). Postmodernists prefer small or community-based narratives that tend not to claim truth and certainty (Rosenau, 1991: 84). Deconstruction, though understood in myriad complex ways, is for our purposes the propensity to seek out what is missing in the text and while doing so to avoid absolute acceptance or rejection of the text as it stands.

Third, pastiche. As postmodernists are concerned pastiche is a practice in confusion and chaos—as sort of free-form improvisation reflective of and contributing to the postmodern landscape.

Fourth, logocentrism. This means of thought is anti-positivistic, thereby undermining knowledge claims steeped in established ways of doing things. Logocentric systems claim legitimacy by invoking some external or higher authority.

It total, "post-modernism in all its forms shakes us loose of our preconceptions (Rosenau, 1991: 169)."

*Burning Sh*t*

In Odd Futures sketch comedy show Loiter Squad a skit (Tori, 2019) involves Tyler the Creator hopping out of a car to greet two disabled young men. He approaches the one in a wheelchair and asks "how do you keep your shoes from gettin' creased," and the guy in the wheelchair replies jovially, "I don't really walk, yea.." and directly following this, in a most playful manner, Tyler jumps on the back of the young man, grabs the back of his wheelchair and pushes him out in front of a moving vehicle, where he is presumably killed. Tyler then, without missing a beat turns to the second man (who is wearing leg braces) and asks him, "Can you hit your Dougie?" (a commonly known dance). The second disabled man attempts this and promptly falls to the ground as Tyler laughs. The next frame has Tyler pop up on the screen proclaiming "I do what I want!" before the next skit begins.

The skit began with what we know of as the politically correct position of acceptance for the disabled, and this carries on though the off-color remark about the shoes, taken in stride by the first disabled man. But this is quickly followed by a callous murder, and thus the skit served to implode a formerly comforting narrative of greater acceptance for the disabled. By killing the young man in the wheelchair OF is expressing distain for the given frame of acceptable behavior by jarring us back into a world where there is no right way to behave and all interactions are risky and subject to unknown outcomes—a postmodern landscape.

The chorus of the song Radicals shouts the following:

> Kill people, burn shit, fuck school
> I'm fuckin' radical, nigga
> Left, right, left, right
> (Okonma, 2011)

The reading of these lyrics should proceed with caution, as the presenters themselves open the song with a disclaimer of sorts explaining that the song is "fucking fiction," and following with "If anything happens, don't fuckin' blame me, white America, fuck Bill O'Reilly." We can see this brutish chorus as a disruption of the narrative that one may embrace of the OF collective as playful and intelligent young men. It is an allusion to gangsta' rap while at the same time, with the use of the word "radical," a skate culture infused declaration of defiance. The left, right, left, right, might be an allusion to a greater ambivalence, perhaps in political positions. As a whole the endeavor itself is a narrative disruption reminding the listener that OF is contradiction filled, both sweet and radical, violent and, in other places, caring.

Finally, consider the song Sandwitches where we hear Tyler say the following:

> "Who the fuck invited Mr. I don't give a fuck
> Who cries about his daddy and a blog because his music sucks? (I did!)
> Well, you fucking up, and truthfully I had enough
> And fuck rolling papers, I'm a rebel, bitch, I'm ashing blunts (Sorry)
> Full of shit, like I ate that John
> Come on kids, fuck that class and hit that bong
> Lets by guns and kill those kids with dads and mom
> With nice homes, 41ks, and nice ass lawns
> Those privileged fucks got to learn that we ain't taking no shit
> Like Ellen Degeneres clitoris is play with dick
> I'm jealous as shit, cause I ain't got no home meal to come to
> So, if you do, I'm throwing fingers out screaming 'fuck you.'"
> (Okonma & Long, 2011)

With this lyric we see the pendulum swing from vulnerability, Tyler admitting to crying about his absent father and bad music reviews, to musings about school shootings and class warfare, and back to personal jealousy and relative deprivation. This too is a type of implosion, where absurdity is applied strategically. Tyler and his mates are engaging in fantasy here, but arising from their lived experience. Closing out the verse Tyler warns:

It's an Odd Future: Deviant Play and the Postmodern | 31

> "Chronic youth, I'm shoving blunt wraps in bitches ovaries
> Punches to the stomach where that bastard kid supposed to be
> Fuck a mask, I want that ho to know it's me, ugh." (Okonma &
> Long, 2011)

It is not acceptable to reflect on, ponder, muse about, joke about, or otherwise consider assaulting women. It is not done. But for OF, this is another boundary to transgress, another "do not skate here" sign to ignore. Such lyrics from the early work of Tyler the Creator and Odd Future actually led to a perception of the group that got them banned from New Zealand where they were said to be "a potential threat to public order" (Walker, 2014) as well as the United Kingdom where she stated that the lyrics "encourage violence and intolerance of homosexuality (Kornhaber, Spencer July 21, 2017)."

Sexual Preference

> "I'm going harder than coming out the closet to conservative Christian
> fathers." (Okonma & Weems, 2015)

Following are some examples of what most perceive to be a term of slander directed at gays:

> "Child support ain't some that faggot still ain't bought me anything."
> (Okonma, 2011)

> "I know you think I'm crazy, Cause I think you're a fucking fag."
> (Okonma, 2013)

> "I'll crash that fucking airplane that that faggot nigga B.o.B is in," and,
> "I'm stabbing any blogging faggot hipster with a Pitchfork, Still suicidal I
> am." (Okonma, 2011)

And here we have a more statements about the issue:

> "I slipped myself some pink Xannies, And danced around the house in all-over
> print panties. My mom's gone, that fucking broad will never understand me,
> I'm not gay, I just want to boogie to some Marvin." (Okonma, 2011)

> "Next line I'll have em' like whoa, I've been kissing white boys since
> 2004." (Okonma, 2017)

Later work by Tyler the Creator, by some accounts the entirely of his album "Flower Boy," is about coming to terms with a gay identity. The earlier work of the artist is certainly more hostile and homophobic though there is no indication from him that it was intended as such. The popular media response to the transition of Tyler, from someone apparently hostile to gays to someone admittedly queer himself, is to see it as a somewhat ironic progression towards enlightenment. Perhaps Tyler fits the bill of another closeted queer person lashing out before he was able to reconcile his true identity. But I contend this may only be partially true, if at all. Youths in a postmodern era are more likely to accept fluidity of gender and sexual preference. OF lays out extremes of violence, passivity, playfulness, aggressiveness, straight/gay, masculine/feminine, all as part of a grander pastiche. Identities and acts appear as scenes and images that exist momentarily only to morph into various other notions. Therefore, I would not be surprised if Tyler is again, just as a skater would, carving his way through a stodgy environment, trying out different moves, and seeing what happens with each new trick. As for the *real* reality of sexual identity, well, that probably never mattered all that much anyway, if it can be seen to exist at all.

Expanded Masculinity and (A)typical Behavior

Another Loiter Squad skit (Adult Swim, 2014) presented as an infomercial asks, "Are you soft-spoken?" "If so you need Ultimate Hypeman!" Ultimate Hypeman is advertised as 6'3" of hype available for corporate meetings, rap battles, and bar mitzvahs. A young black male, Earl Sweatshirt, is next seen meekly presenting a profitability report in a typical office meeting environment while a table of all-white coworker's mocks and dismisses him. But then, on call, Ultimate Hypeman appears as a superhero of sorts demanding attention from the all-white audience and in turn elevating the status of the soft-spoken young man.

It is the invocation of the Ultimate Hypeman that gives validity to the claims made by the young soft-spoken man, not the content of what he is saying. OF recognizes that the messenger rather than the message is what people respond to. As such logocentric systems are brought into question and undermined in favor of the lived experience of its not what you say, it's how loudly and confidently you say it. The brash braggadocio that Hypman brings to bear is reminiscent of the typical rapper and a more typical presentation of black masculinity. OF, by presenting this character, is both playing with and reflecting upon the various ways black men communicate and how that communication in perceived. Ultimately OF deconstructs these two specific modes, the soft-spoken and the brash, thereby imploding each.

In the song "Running out of the Time," Tyler opines:

> "So, take your mask off, I need it out the picture
> Take your mask off, stop lyin' for these niggas
> Stop lyin' to yourself, I know the real you

> Halloween ain't for a minute, lose the costume
> You need to chill, OK
> Been running from the targets and them back in the day"
> (Okonma, 2019)

The lyrics seems to be intended as a plea for the attention of a lover, one that calls for the shedding of pretext, particularly the "mask" or "costume." The costume could be understood as a ready-made role, image, or *reel* (*See* Assante Jr. 2008) that African Americans are expected to adopt. The reel of course includes a hyper-masculine presentation, very much like the Ultimate Hypeman depicted above. There are many such lyrics, in the work of Tyler the Creator specifically, that present a soft or even feminine outlook. It is noteworthy that in hip-hop culture this is not a new development, but it is one that has been accentuated in the era of alternative hip-hop defined by Odd Future. For OF, the lived experience is that of skateboard brats, and everything they depict, although real on some level, is primarily simulation, or allusion to previous claims to truth, only existing momentarily outside of the flooded marketplace of images and ideas.

Conclusion

> "African American identity is not unitary but plural, fluid not fixed; it can be politically useful or constraining and dysfunctional, a haven from white racism or a source of self-loathing." (Jones 2007: 668)

Subcultural activity, as a postmodern act, set OF on a career of creative deconstruction and playful production, first as rappers, and later through various creative endeavors. I argue that the act of skateboarding, as a deviant act, served to solidify a particular outcast identity for these young people. The act of skating itself, carving through the landscape and defying authority in the process, was pre-socialization for their future careers and professional trouble-makers. The marginalization they experienced was both a curse and a privilege leading one naturally to a place of critique, questioning the judgment of others and gaining the will to judge for oneself.

OF developed in a post-modern age where essentialisms are antiquated. The postmodern elements in their music, style, and affect in part explain their popularity. The artifacts here can be read as evidence that a shift of some sort beyond modernism has likely occurred. It is also noteworthy that there are many other artists exhibiting such themes, both today, and less so in the recent past. Interestingly the outsiders have increasingly become insiders to a degree. This was made most evident in 2019, when concertgoers at Tyler the Creators Camp Flog Gnaw festival booed the surprise headliner, multiple

Grammy award winner Drake, throughout his performance. Rumor had it that OF member Frank Ocean was going to perform and the crowd voiced their disappointment to the dismay of the rap community. Even Tyler himself expressed his displeasure with fans, perhaps because the spectacle threatened to undermine the collectives' outsider status. Tyler the Creator's fans may have just made him bigger than Drake.

Ultimately by broadening what it means to be a rapper these black artists served to liberate a new generation from what MK Assante Jr. called the *Reel*, a false image serving a white industry and promoting limiting images of black people. Researchers and critics tend to focus on the negative aspects of deviance in hip-hop culture overall. But what we see with Odd Future is the story of how beneficial a certain brand of deviance can be. This is a story of some black kids getting to experience an outsider or deviant status while not being summarily dismissed and discarded as has been the experience of so many black youths at the foot of the racial hierarchy. White middle-class youth have the freedom to engage in deviant practices and turn those practices into lucrative careers—in part because law enforcement is less likely to trap white youths you deviate within the criminal justice apparatus. In short, it is a luxury to be able to experiment with deviance, it nurtures creativity and builds confidence. With alternative hip-hop some black youths can finally enjoy these benefits of deviant play.

References

Adult Swim. (2014). "Ultimate Hypeman: Meetings/Loiter Squad/Adult Swim." Video 1:00. https://www.youtube.com/watch?v=MyYbIseMYZc

Assante Jr, M. K. (2008). It's bigger than hip hop. *The rise of the Post-Hip-Hop-Generation*. New York.

Baudrillard, J. (1983). Simulations. New York: Semiotext (e).

Becker Howard, S. (1963). Outsiders. *Studies in the sociology of deviance.*

Beato, G. (2007). The lords of Dogtown. *Youth subcultures: Exploring underground America* (pp. 160–170).

Gramsci, A. (1971). Selections from the Prison Notebooks, ed. and trans. Quintin Hoare and Geoffrey Nowell Smith.

Haenfler, R. (2014). *Subcultures: The basics*. Routledge.

Hooper, G. (2012). A popular postmodern or a postmodern popular?. *International Review of the Aesthetics and Sociology of Music*, 187–207.

Lefebvre, H., & Nicholson-Smith, D. (1991). *The production of space* (Vol. 142). Blackwell: Oxford.

Jones, D. M. (2007). Postmodernism, pop music, and blues practice in Nelson George's post-soul culture. *African American Review*, 41(4), 667–694.

Kornhaber, S. (2017). The classic Queer Paradox of Tyler, the Creator. Retrieved from https://www.theatlantic.com/entertainment/archive/2017/07/tyler-the-creator-flower-boy-coming-out-queerness/534486/

Lyng, S. (1990). Edgework: A social psychological analysis of voluntary risk taking. *American Journal of Sociology*, 95(4), 851–886.

Lyotard, J.F., & Thébaud, J.L. (1985). Just gaming (W. Godzich, Trans.). Minneapolis, MN.

Molokov, K., & Zueva, E. (2017). Rap poetry and postmodernism. *Journal of History Culture and Art Research*, 6(4), 1358–1364.

Okonma, T. (2011). Radicals [song]. On Goblin. XL.

Okonma, T. (2011). Yonkers [song]. On Goblin. XL.

Okonma, T. (2013). Wolf [song]. Wolf. Odd Future.

Okonma, T. (2017). I Aint Got Time [song]. Flower Boy. Columbia Records.

Okonma, T. (2019). Running Out of Time [song]. IGOR. Columbia Records..

Okonma, T., & Long, G. (2011). Sandwitches [song]. On Goblin. XL.

Okonma, T., & Weems, H. (2015). Deathcamp [song]. Cherry Bomb. Odd Future.

Pfohl, S. J. (1994). *Images of deviance and social control: A sociological history* (p. 2). New York: McGraw-Hill.

Potter, R.A. (1995). *Spectacular vernaculars: Hip-hop and the politics of postmodernism*. SUNY Press.

Quinney, R. (1975). *Criminology: Analysis and critique of crime in America*.

Reiman, J., & Leighton, P. (2010). *Rich get richer and the poor get prison, the (subscription): Ideology, class, and criminal justice*. Routledge.

Rosenau, P. M. (1991). *Post-modernism and the social sciences: Insights, inroads, and intrusions*. Princeton University Press.

Rundquist, R. (2007). Street skateboarding and the government stamp of approval. *Youth Subcultures: Exploring Underground America*, 179–189.

Smith, D. (2013). *Zygmunt Bauman: prophet of postmodernity*. John Wiley & Sons.

Tori. (2019). A really long loiter squad compilation. [video]. 24:52. https://www.youtube.com/watch?v=kXEyIjTYMmU&list=PL3UhXd_Dr6mvGzRPnWvvIDv4ff5tNPlfN

Walker, B. (2014). New Zealand refuses entry to rap group Odd Future. Retrieved from https://www.cnn.com/2014/02/13/world/asia/new-zealand-odd-future-ban/index.html

Thug Life: Hip-Hop's Curious Relationship with Criminal Justice[1]

ANDRÉ DOUGLAS POND CUMMINGS[*]

I. Introduction

Hip-hop music and culture profoundly influence attitudes toward, and perceptions about, criminal justice in the United States. At base, hip-hop lyrics and their cultural accoutrements turn U.S. punishment philosophy on its head, effectively defeating the foundational purposes of crime and punishment. Prison and punishment philosophy in the United States is based on clear principles of retribution and incapacitation, where prison time for crime should serve to deter individuals from engaging in criminal behavior. In addition, the stigma that attaches to imprisonment should dissuade criminals from recidivism. Hip-hop culture denounces crime and punishment in the United States by defying the underlying penal philosophy adopted and championed by legislators for decades. Since the inception of hip-hop as a musical genre, hip-hop artists have rhymed in a narrative format that starkly informs listeners and fans that the entire fundamental regime of prison for crime in the United States is suspect, illegitimate, and profane.

Because U.S. criminal law and punishment are profane and illegitimate to many, as hip-hop artists historically and fiercely argue,[2] two of the primary foundational underpinnings of the criminal justice system are lost on the "hip-hop generation"[3]: deterrence and stigma. "When incarceration is not sufficiently stigmatized, it loses its value as deterrence."[4]

Professor Paul Butler powerfully notes in his ground-breaking 2009 book, Let's Get Free: A Hip-Hop Theory of Justice, that despite the apparent divide between socially conscious rap and gangsta rap, the hip-hop artists and culture agree profoundly on one thing: that overwhelming inequities permeate the criminal justice system in the United States.[5] And hip-hop harshly critiques crime and punishment inequality in our country.[6] Because, as hip-hop aggressively describes, crime and punishment in the United States is fundamentally unfair, inequitable, and biased against people of color and the poor,[7] punishment for committing certain crimes here is viewed by the hip-hop nation as illegitimate, and imprisonment for committing suspect crimes is unaffecting.[8] Hip-hop culture has engendered in the global hip-hop generation a tradition of exposing racial inequality and social injustice, particularly within the United States.[9]

This article will begin by exploring the global ascent of hip-hop music through an examination of how it has influenced an entire generation towards a deep distrust of the criminal justice system in the United States, to the point where imprisonment is respected, if not lauded, and deterrence has lost any realistic value for those who engage in "criminal" behavior.[10] After examining hip-hop "lessons" through rhyme and baseline, the article will focus on the political agenda of early rap artists that included clear messages of defiance and deep disrespect for a criminal justice regime that systematically targeted young African American and urban youth.[11] Then, this piece explores what it means for a hip-hop generation to come of age while retaining chasm-like differences from the traditional majority perspective on crime and punishment in the United States, and how this development will impact punishment and justice in this country going forward.[12]

II. A Global Footprint

Hip-hop music and culture have "conquered" the world.[13] Since hip-hop's humble beginnings in the streets and parks of the South Bronx in New York City, it has, in just thirty years, become a United States phenomenon and a global cultural and entertainment movement.[14] Hip-hop artists regularly top American and international record sales charts.[15] Motion pictures with hip-hop themes chart regularly on box office reports, both in the United States and internationally.[16] Hip-hop artists have become record moguls,[17] international movie stars,[18] clothing designers,[19] stars of reality television programming,[20] and world renowned collaborators.[21] Hip-hop studies programs have sprung up throughout the undergraduate educational academy[22] and a burgeoning body of literature has documented this global ascent.[23] In a relatively short period of time, hip hop has become a dominant cultural force and, in many ways, has become the voice of a generation.[24]

This global movement, however, sprang from very humble roots. Rap music and hip-hop culture was dismissed at its inception as a fad and was widely panned by critics and many in the general public as an unimportant "flash in the pan" musical movement.[25] The public seemed content to ignore hip-hop and its accoutrements (i.e., break dancing, graffiti, deejaying, etc.) when the movement was confined to the inner city of major U.S. metropolises.[26] Thus, when the 1970s and 1980s saw the Sugar Hill Gang release *Rapper's Delight*, Afrika Bambaataa release *Planet Rock*, Kurtis Blow release *Basketball* and *If I Ruled the World*, and Whodini release *Five Minutes of Funk*, legislators and law enforcement paid little heed to this nascent movement.

However, when in the 1980s, hip-hop began creeping into the cassette players and minds of white American suburban youth—particularly with aggressive, violent, and counter culture lyrics—the general public, its legislators, and law enforcement began to take urgent notice.[27] When Public Enemy released *It Takes a Nation of Millions to Hold Us Back* and *Fear of a Black Planet*, featuring *Don't Believe the Hype*, *Black Steel in the Hour of Chaos*, *Fight the Power*, and *911 is a Joke;* when N.W.A. released *Straight Outta Compton*, featuring *Fuck Tha Police* and *Gangsta Gangsta;* when Boogie Down Productions and KRS-One released *Criminal Minded* and *By All Means Necessary;* and when Ice-T released singles *6 in the Mornin'* and *Cop Killer*, hip-hop suddenly became a lightning rod for attention and criticism.[28] New and aggressive critiques labeled hip-hop as dangerous, irresponsible, and certain to lead listeners to violence while potentially upsetting the fragile balance of law and order in minority communities. This newfound status as controversial lightning rod came to be, not just because of the explicit political and violent counter culture messages, but because these messages were being *heard* and received widely by inner city youth and also by white suburban youth across the country.[29] In addition, as Professor Andre Smith argues, hip-hop openly defied traditional property laws across the board, including intellectual property and municipal property codes.[30] Early hip-hop's civil disobedience took the form of house parties and park performances held without required permits or payment for electricity, unlicensed radio stations known as "pirate stations" playing hip-hop across the country, music sampling, and illegal production and distribution of records and tapes.[31]

Despite intense criticism and attempts to discredit and eradicate hip-hop music, including aggressive attacks launched by the FBI,[32] CIA, local law enforcement across the United States,[33] Tipper Gore,[34] and C. Delores Tucker,[35] hip-hop has not just survived, but has influenced and dominated a generation—the hip-hop generation.[36] One commentator notes: "Hip-Hop has assumed a central role in molding the destinies of a whole generation of young people."[37] Simply stated, hip-hop music and its counter culture exploded upon U.S. and global consciousness.

From the 1980s through today, hip-hop culture has grown in its power and influence. Debate has raged during these three decades as to whether hip-hop's influence has been a positive force or a destructive mechanism, but few still believe or argue that hip-hop will fade to a mere cultural footnote.

The genuine power and robust influence of hip-hop and its generation was on clear display during the 2008 presidential election. President Barack Obama was fueled to victory in the historic 2008 election by many various supporting constituencies; one of the most important, which drove Obama to the most powerful position in the world, was the hip-hop generation.[38] Socially conscious rapper Talib Kweli backed and campaigned for President Obama, and referred to him as not just the first black President, but the first hip-hop President.[39] NPR reported: "Rappers like Lil' Wayne, Young Jeezy, Jay-Z and Nas rallied their fans behind President-elect Barack Obama's campaign. And like their hip-hop forefathers, the kings and queens of rap preached about social justice, the economy and the power of democracy."[40] Dr. Cornel West, when reflecting upon the historic campaign waged by Barack Obama for the presidency of the United States, recently mused:

> I would go as far as to suggest that there is a good chance that there wouldn't even be an "Age of Obama" without hip-hop, given the fundamental role that young people played in galvanizing the whole campaign. I was there in Iowa when there was just a few of us. Disproportionately young, disproportionately white and when we stole away they were all listening to hip-hop. And I am not talking about just EminemHip-hop doing what? Opening young people to the humanity of other young black people whose conditions have been overlooked.[41]

At bottom, as hip-hop has become the voice of a generation, and recognizing the sizeable global footprint that hip-hop has created, two things seem clear: first, as the hip-hop nation emerges, some of its members will become leaders, including legislators, educators, lawyers, scholars, and philosophers; and second, these leaders and educators will bring the images, lessons, and stark critiques that accompany all authentic members of this generation into their leadership roles. Because hip-hop is deeply impacting an emerging generation of leaders and scholars, society should pay very close attention to the messages and lessons that hip-hop has taught and continues to teach its generation.

Particular awareness should be paid to the one lesson upon which all of hip-hop, both "gangsta" and "socially conscious," seems to agree: that the United States system of crime and punishment is inequitable, unfairly administered, and purposely aimed to disempower people of color and the voiceless.

III. "The Educational Level I'm Giving the People"[42]

While many different iterations exist in the world of hip-hop music and culture, a common division often cited is that between socially conscious hip-hop and the hip-hop that focuses on violence, misogyny, and gaining riches ("Wing" or "gangsta rap"), which permeates much of what is currently released for public consumption.[43] While this differentiation may be too simplistic, many commentators agree that some type of divide exists in hip-hop between that which is positive and uplifts the black and inner city community (socially conscious rap) and that which is negative and serves to degrade women, perpetuate violence, maintain stereotypes, and injure the black and inner city community (bling or gangsta rap).[44] One reason that this characterization is too simple is that many "gangsta" rappers release records that could be characterized as positive and uplifting, while many "socially conscious" rappers release music that could be characterized as misogynistic or violent.[45] As Professor Pamela Bridgewater has noted, hip-hop refuses to apologize for the many and often complex inconsistencies it portrays.[46] Still, very early on, both socially conscious hip-hop artists and gangsta rappers began to understand the power and influence they could wield in "molding the destinies" of hip-hop's fans and adherents. In the 1980s, "socially conscious" rap stars KRS-One and Public Enemy began articulating clear messages to the public/fans, with albums like *Edutainment*[47] and songs like *Fight the Power*.[48] Hip-hop stars became keenly aware of their burgeoning influence and many took it upon themselves to educate the hip-hop generation.

Hip-hop legend Tupac Shakur recognized this influence when he boldly stated: "I guarantee that I will spark the brain that will change the world."[49] Gangsta rap pioneer Ice-T described this flourishing influence in particularly savvy terms when responding to critics of his stark realist hip-hop lyrics by boldly proclaiming that the hip-hop stars of the 1980s and 1990s would truly influence a nation:

> They are not really after me for that, [law enforcement and critics are] after me because of the educational level I'm giving the people. And I'm telling them, I am giving them the guts to say, "Fuck em." See, this is what scares them. They are scared of one brother yelling out "the system can 'kiss my ass.'" This could cause a problem.
>
> They are also afraid of the fact that kids that go to law schools, Harvard and all these, are listening to my album, think its dope and these kids are the next ones that are going to be sitting on the Supreme Court. Next, what you are going to have in five years is that the Supreme Court is going to be wearing Too Short, Ice-T, Yo-Yo, Ice Cube t-shirts. The country will be fucked, as far as they're concerned. I think it will be a great place.[50]

Like Ice-T, Professor Smith not only recognizes the influence that hip-hop artists have in educating America's hip-hop generation, he also opines that these artists have influenced the perspectives of listeners across the world:

> For many of the world's poor and non-propertied, the emergence of hip-hop culture has represented a powerful movement against the propertied and the social order maintaining their wealth. Surely, Public Enemy's song "Fight the Power" promoted hip-hop globally as an art form capable and worthy of adoption by those struggling for economic or social justice
>
> [I]t is not surprising that, for example, young Palestinian and Brazilian youths have embraced hip-hop as their way of expressing dissatisfaction with their social order, as do rebellious suburban teenagers in the U.S.[51]

As hip-hop has roared to an ever increasing apex in connection with its power, influence, and global impact, and as hip-hop artists recognize this influence and impact, it would behoove the traditional majority to sit up and recognize what this global genre is saying about crime, punishment, inequality, and imprisonment in the United States and across the world.

IV. *What HIP-HOP Teaches About Crime, punishment, and Imprisonment*

Recently, hip-hop superstar Lil' Wayne delivered a rap message that should motivate the traditional majority to "sit up and recognize." Lil' Wayne released the song "Don't Get It" in 2008 which included the following critique of the U.S. system of punishment:

> I'm just a soul whose intentions are good
> Oh lord please don't let me be misunderstood.
> I was watching T.V. the other day right
> Got this white guy up there talking about black guys Talking about how young black guys are targeted Targeted by who? America
> You see one in every 100 Americans are locked up
> One in every 9 black Americans are locked up
> And see what the white guy was trying to stress was that The money we spend on sending a mothafucka to jail A young mothafucka to jail
> Would be less to send his or her young ass to college
> See, and another thing the white guy was stressing was that
> Our jails are populated with drug dealers, you know crack/cocaine stuff like that
> Meaning due to the laws we have on crack/cocaine and regular cocaine
> Police are only, I don't want to say only right, but shit Only logic by riding around in the hood all day And not in the suburbs
> Because crack cocaine is mostly found in the hood
> And you know the other thing is mostly found in... you know where I'm going
> But why bring a mothafucka to jail if it's not gon' stand up in court

Thug Life: Hip-Hop's Curious Relationship   13

> Cause, this drug ain't that drug, you know level 3, level 4 drug, shit like that
> I guess it's all a misunderstanding
> I sit back and think, you know us young mothafuckas you know that 1 in 9
> We probably only selling the crack cocaine because we in the hood
> And it's not like in the suburbs, we don't have what you have
> Why? I really don't wanna know the answer I guess we just misunderstood, hunh
> You know we don't have room in the jails now for the real mothafuckas, the real criminals
> Sex offenders, rapists, serial killers Don't get scared, don't get scared[52]

Thus, in 2008, millions of Lil' Wayne fans either learned or were reminded of both the excruciatingly unfair crack versus cocaine sentencing laws in the United States and of the inequitable prison sentencing numbers that continue to destroy the inner city. For example, when Lil' Wayne rhymes about "1 in 100 Americans being locked up" but "1 in 9 black Americans being locked up," he reminds hip-hop aficionados andteachesamateur hip-hoplistenersabout the incomprehensible incarceration bias against African Americans in the United States.[53] When Lil' Wayne raps that it is "only logic" for police to infiltrate "the hood" daily based on the cocaine versus crack sentencing disparity, he reminds the hip-hop enlightened and teaches budding hip-hop fans that the United States Congress has, for twenty years, perpetuated a racist and biased sentencing disparity between drug users and dealers that traffic cocaine (typically white suburban users—punished lightly) versus crack cocaine (typically minority inner city users—punished severely).[54]

Lil' Wayne in *Don't Get It* simply propagates the hip-hop tradition of using lyric and wide audience appeal to educate the hip-hop generation. Harsh critique of the inequities in the criminal justice system and police brutality was on early display in N.W.A's 1989 *Fuck Tha Police:*

> Fuck the police
> Comin straight from the underground
> Young n***a got it bad cuz I'm brown
> And not the other color so police think
> They have the authority to kill a minority
>
> Fuck that shit, cuz I ain't tha one
> For a punk mothafucka with a badge and a gun To be beatin on, and thrown in jail
> We can go toe to toe in the middle of a cell
>
> Fuckin' with me cuz I'm a teenager
> With a little bit of gold and a pager
> Searchin my car, lookin for the product Thinkin every n***a is sellin narcotics
>
> You'd rather see me in the pen
> Than me and Lorenzo rollin' in the Benzo

> And on the other hand, without a gun they can't get none But don't let it be a black and white one
>
> Cuz they'll slam ya down to the street top Black police showin' out for the white cop
>
> Ice Cube will swarm
> On any mothafucka in a blue uniform
> Just cuz I'm from the CPT, punk police are afraid of me, huh
> A young n***a on the warpath
> And when I'm finished, it's gonna be a bloodbath Of cops dyin' in L.A.
> Yo, Dre, I got something to say[55]

As in 2008 with Lil' Wayne and *Don't Get It,* when N.W.A. released the furiously defiant *Fuck Tha Police* in 1989, a generation of young people were instructed that law enforcement routinely targets minority youth *expecting* most to be involved in drug trafficking and that the criminal justice system often *prefers* that young African American youth be installed in jails and prisons, whether guilty of crime or not.[56] At that time, the 1980s, this exposed notion of targeting, profiling, and preferred imprisonment of inner city youth for "soft crime,"[57] and the clarion call for defiance in response to this unjust system, was audacious and stunning in its raw, starkly realized exposé. Law enforcement, together with the traditional majority, reacted swiftly in an attempt to stifle and silence this critique.[58] The FBI famously penned a missive to N.W.A.'s record label protesting the content of the group's music, while Public Enemy faced constant media criticism, including charges of anti-Semitism and reckless black militancy.[59]

A. Hip-Hop Lessons

Beginning in the 1980s with Public Enemy, KRS-One, N.W.A., and Ice-T among many others, hip-hop artists began describing, in stark rhymes and narratives, a United States criminal justice system that was inequitable and unfair, a system that targets and profiles African-Americans and inner city youth, and the descriptions by those artists became, in Chuck D's words, "the Black CNN."[60] As discussed in Part III, these rap artists *knew* that they were the Black CNN and were influencing and molding a generation. Hip-hop's musical tradition is to be, in many instances, black America's first response to current inequities and discriminations. As Professor Mark Anthony Neal stated: "Whether it's Katrina three years ago, the L.A. riots in 1992, Jesse Jackson's run [in] 1984, you know, hip-hop was seen as black America's first response.[61]

In *Much Respect,* Professor Butler writes:

Thug Life: Hip Hop's Curious Relationship 45

> At the same time that an art form created by African American and Latino men dominates popular culture, African American and Latino men dominate American prisons. Unsurprisingly then, justice—especially criminal justice—has been a preoccupation of the hip-hop nation. The culture contains a strong descriptive and normative analysis of punishment by the people who know it best.[62]

Thus, a movement that was beginning to dominate a generation, combined with artists who understood the potential dominance and who lived on the front lines of the crime and punishment system in the United States, came together in a perfect storm of platform, audience, and defiance. The hip-hop generation was going to learn, in no uncertain terms, about the inequities, injustices, and discriminations in the U.S. criminal justice system.

> Hip-hop exposes the current punishment regime as profoundly unfair. It demonstrates this view by, if not glorifying law breakers, at least not viewing all criminals with disgust which the law seeks to attach to them. Hip-hop points out the incoherence of the law's construct of crime, and it attacks the legitimacy of the system. Its message has the potential to transform justice in the United States.[63]

In the 1980s and 1990s, hip-hop stars described, to their eager audiences, including millions of suburban white youths, the inequities in criminal law and punishment, including (a) the specific targeting of inner city communities, revealed by the now well-known massive prison population disparity (nearly 60 % of men imprisoned for drug offenses are African American, while only 12 % of the total U.S. population is black);[64] (b) the egregiously unfair imprisonment of inner city crack dealers versus suburban cocaine dealers, revealed by the well-known crack/cocaine sentencing disparity (prison time for a crack seller or taker is 100 times greater than prison time for a cocaine seller or taker);[65] (c) the American epidemic of police brutality inspired by the "siege mentality" that infests most large police forces, revealed by the well-known brutalizations of Rodney King, Abner Louima, Sean Bell, and others;[66] and (d) the flooding of inner city communities with law enforcement officers, through the "War on Drugs," the "War on Gangs," and the "War on Crime," while suburban crime and white collar crime continued seemingly unhindered and unabated.[67]

In educating the hip-hop generation, Grandmaster Flash and the Furious Five recorded and released *The Message*;[68] Public Enemy famously recorded *Fight the Power*,[69] *Don't Believe the Hype*,[70] *Black Steel in the Hour of Chaos*,[71] and *911 is a Joke*;[72] N.W.A. notoriously released *Fuck Tha Police*,[73] and *100 Miles and Runnin'*;[74] Tupac Shakur released *Brenda's Got a Baby*,[75] *Keep Ya Head Up*,[76] and *To Live & Die in L.A.*;[77] Ice Cube released the explosive

AmeriKKKas Most Wanted,[78] featuring *Endangered Species (Tales from the Darkside)*[79] and later *Dead Homiez*,[80] KRS-One released an entire album he styled *Edutainment*,[81] featuring *Love's Gonna Getcha*.[82] Each release was an effort on the part of the hip-hop artist to educate and enlighten the hip-hop generation, particularly as to the inequities and discriminations inherent in a criminal justice system that systematically targets minority and urban youth.

Today in 2024, carrying the Black CNN torch lit by early hip-hop street reporters are Kendrick Lamar, J. Cole, Lizzo, and Meek Mill who, among others, continue to capture the disaffection that black Americans and urban youth have with a criminal justice system that remains a profiling, targeting, "law enforcement versus the enemy" construct.[83]

In hearing and feeling these lessons dropped by hip-hop educators, an entire hip-hop nation learned and continues to learn a much different system of criminal justice than that what was taught to them in grade school, high school, college, and graduate school, including law school. More than any other lesson learned, perhaps the most striking is that the entire foundational principle of prison for crime in the United States is suspect, illegitimate, and profane.

B. *United States Philosophy of Punishment and Imprisonment*

While varying philosophical under pinnings for punishment and imprisonment are debated worldwide, the prevailing view of imprisonment in the United States is referred to as the "conservative approach" to imprisonment.[84] This "conservatism: deterrence and incapacitation" prizes the philosophy that casting criminals into prison will deter individuals from acting in ways that lead to prison.[85] "Prison life should be uncomfortable—even painful—and rational people will be deterred from committing crime to avoid being sent there again."[86] While some attempts have been made throughout U.S. history to use imprisonment for purposes of rehabilitation, the prevailing view in this country is that prison will deter criminals and the stigma of having been imprisoned will inspire those inclined to crime to avoid criminal behavior and deter them from returning.[87] Deterrence and stigma then serve, in many ways, as the foundational principles for imprisonment in the United States.

Perhaps one of the greatest weaknesses in the current regime of U.S. crime and punishment, and most criticized, is that incarceration and retributivism is fundamentally based on a system that has always been developed from the top down.[88] More plainly stated, the U.S. system of criminal justice has been developed and refined, from inception, by the privileged and the powerful,[89] those individuals who have little to no experience or firsthand knowledge of poverty, despair, voicelessness, and victimization.[90] Hip-hop argues, even philosophizes, about a system of punishment that can and should be developed from the bottom-up.[91]

> Thousands of hip-hop songs consider crime and punishment. These voices are worth listening to—they evaluate criminal justice from the bottom up We might punish better if the ghetto philosophers and the classic philosophers met. They address many of the same issues in punishment, including causation, harm, responsibility, excuse, and justification.[92]

Speaking in broad brush strokes, those that favor imprisonment as a means of deterrent punishment and retribution are those that have inhabited the rare air of the privileged. Those that favor rehabilitation as a means of punishment and imprisonment are typically those who know firsthand, that life is messy, seedy, and rarely as perfect as it is for the privileged.[93]

Because of the top-down approach of crime and punishment in the United States, our prisons are literally teeming with minority convicts who are incarcerated for soft drug crimes,[94] will be imprisoned for decades because of skewed sentencing guidelines,[95] and will share the same cells inhabited by murderers, rapists, pedophiles, and hardened career criminals.[96]

This top-down approach of determining which activity will count as criminal and which will not (i.e., marijuana sale and use—a crime; alcohol and tobacco sale and use—not a crime), of determining which crimes will be severely punished and which will not (i.e., peddling soft drugs and crack— harshly punished; bankrupting corporations and destroying capital markets—not harshly punished, but in fact, bailed out with taxpayers money), and favoring harsh imprisonment with little directed rehabilitative effort, has been recognized in hip-hop music and culture as illegitimate and profane.

C. *The Curious Relationship Between Hip-Hop and Imprisonment*

As described above, to many in the hip-hop generation, U.S. criminal law is profane and illegitimate, as forcefully argued by artists from hip-hop's birth in the Bronx through today.[97] As such, the goals of deterrence, stigma, and incarceration are primarily *lost* on the hip-hop nation. Many in the hip-hop generation recognize that imprisonment, arrest, and charges of criminal activity are little more than politically motivated, incoherent, inefficient, and unworthy directives. Because imprisonment for various crimes is political, incoherent, inefficient, and unworthy, much of the U.S. crime and punishment regime is given no respect by hip-hop culture. Therefore, for many members of the hip-hop nation, prison has come to be viewed as a "rite of passage" and a legitimating activity in the hip-hop hustle.

Over and over, hip-hop artists "shout out" their brothers and sisters in prison, recognizing them as human and worthy of respect and attention. Most know that, in the eyes of those that matter to them, the "brother behind bars" is probably illegitimately incarcerated. Jay Z recognizes this in *"A Ballad For A Fallen Soldier"*:

> Shout to my n****s that's locked up in jail P.O.W's that still in the war for real
> But if he's locked in the penitentiary, send him some energy
> They all winners to me[98]

Ludacris recognizes this in *"Do Your Time"*:

> If you doin' 25 to life, stay up homie
> I got your money on ice, so stay up homie
> If you locked in the box keep makin' it through
> Do your time, do your time, don't let your time do you[99]

T.I. recognizes this in *"You Ain't Missin' Nothin'"*:

> The time'll do itself, all you gotta do is show up Keep layin' down wakin' up
> And thankin' the Lord
> And 'fore you know it they gonna open the doors
>
> I know the times seem long
> Just try and keep strong
> Put on your headphones and rewind this song Remember you ain't missin' nothin' homes I promise you ain't missin' nothin' homes[100]

Many in the hip-hop generation believe, by and large, that the United States has abdicated its responsibility to the poor and those in the 'hood, as evidenced by poverty, lack of opportunity, and joblessness. So much so, that the stigma of being imprisoned for theft, drug crimes, or some violence is simply absent.[101] "Breaking the law is seen as a form of rebelling against the oppressive status quo Rappers who brag about doing time are like old soldiers who boast of war wounds.[102] A commentator further writes: "If imprisonment is no longer viewed primarily as a substantial loss of one's freedom and liberty to be avoided, but rather a rite of passage resulting in increased social respect, can we really expect individuals to fear or respect the law?"[103] As imprisonment in the United States is viewed by many as a rite of passage and the prisoner is viewed with respect and admiration, and as the value of deterrence is diluted and stigma is lost on the hip-hop generation, should not then a new American theory of crime, punishment, and imprisonment be considered and implemented?

Crime and punishment in the United States is predicated on deterrence, incapacitation, and stigmatization, and the hip-hop generation recognizes none as truly legitimate. The system of crime and punishment in the United

States has lost its way. The criminal justice system is disrespected and dismissed by a wide swath of American citizens. This should be a chilling and sobering thought to legislators, prosecutors, judges, and lawmakers.[104]

This is not to say that hip-hop ignores law-breaking or does not believe in some type of retributive consequence for engaging in immoral crimes. It recognizes the need for imprisonment for legitimate crime and seeks community retribution for crimes like murder, rape, child abuse, and so forth.[105] But as for the illegitimate or inequitable punishment for crimes, including drug crimes and sentencing, the three-strikes laws, and the loitering and petty theft crimes, these are all viewed as skewed against people of color and imprisonment for these crimes are ignored, dismissed as illegitimate, and disavowed. Hip-hop culture recognizes that in many instances, crime is justified by lack of opportunity.[106] As Professor Butler cogently recognizes: "Hip-hop culture emphasizes the role of environment in determining conduct, whereas classic retributivist theory focuses on individual choice. In essence, hip-hop culture discounts responsibility when criminal conduct has been shaped by a substandard environment."[107]

The question I am most interested in seeing answered is this: will the emerging leaders of the hip-hop generation—including lawyers, scholars, legislators, economists, preachers, laborers, and teachers radically change the broken system of crime, imprisonment, and punishment in the United States?

One scholar has started on this path already by suggesting six ways that hip-hop can assist in producing legitimate standards of crime and punishment in the United States, a regime that respects the individual, protects the community, and imprisons only those from whom society needs protection. For the hip-hop generation legislator or policy maker, Professor Butler, from a hip-hop perspective, offers a starting place for a more humane, more bottom-up approach to crime and punishment in the United States:

> First, the purpose of punishment should be retribution. Second, punishment should be limited (but not determined) by utilitarian concerns, especially the effect of punishment on people other than the lawbreaker. Third, punishment should be designed to "catch" the harm caused by rich people more than poor people. Fourth, people probably should not be punished for using or selling intoxicants. Fifth, punishment should be imposed only by people within a community, not outsiders. Sixth, prison should be used sparingly as an instrument of punishment.[108]

Will those emerging leaders from within the hip-hop nation respond to this call?

V. Conclusion

Hip-hop teaches that the U.S. system of crime and punishment is inequitable, and does so primarily by exposing, in stark lyric and behavior, that the poor are punished more harshly than the rich, and that drug offenders are punished more harshly than white collar criminals. An amazing chasm exists between the hip-hop generation and the traditional majority perspectives. Hip-hop asks who the true criminals are: young inner city youth selling drugs with no prospects for work, petty thieves stealing to eat, or the 2008 corporate executives at MG, Lehman Brothers, Countrywide, and Bear Stearns, who recklessly torpedoed the U.S. economy and, rather than facing jail, received government bailout money exceeding $800 billion dollars.[109] Hip-hop adjudges this system of prioritizing crime in this way as obscene.

Respected scholars are arguing today that hip-hop offers a legitimate alternative theory of justice,[110] that hip-hop's bold trespass into traditional copyright and property law is a form of civil disobedience,[111] that hip-hop has influenced a generation of law students and young lawyers to proactively seek radical means of justice,[112] that hip-hop comfortably debates and exposes the "dark side" of American society and inequality,[113] that gangsta rappers stake an important place in the black public sphere while still providing seeds of political expression amidst the violence and misogyny,[114] that criminal prosecution of mix-tape DJs is an improper use of police power in an ever changing copyright dynamic,[115] that hip-hop did not create the violence and misogyny rampant within it but merely contextualized it for the black community,[116] and that hip-hop profoundly influences political discourse.[117] It then seems time for U.S. legislators and policy makers to reexamine the fundamental underpinnings of crime and punishment in the United States. It simply does not work for the hip-hop generation.

Hip-hop erases the stigma of imprisonment. Hip-hop refuses to acknowledge the deterrent power of the U.S. prison system as it recognizes the many illegitimate and profane uses of the law to subjugate people of color and punish the poor and powerless, while ignoring the criminal behavior of the wealthy and privileged. While hip-hop does not say much about actual life in prison, it certainly respects the imprisoned and welcomes the convicted back into society openly.

If in fact, American society is no longer fine with its prisons overflowing with petty criminals and grossly disproportionate imprisonment of minorities, and if American citizens are no longer fine with spending billions of dollars on building prisons, while cutting billions of dollars from education,[118] then perhaps a new nascent movement is afoot—one that will radically alter the course of crime and punishment in the United States.

Notes

1 Portions of the following chapter, first appeared in 50 Santa Clara L. Rev. 515 (2010).
* Dean Designate, Widener University Commonwealth Law School; Associate Dean for Faculty Research & Development, Charles C. Baum Professor of Law, and Co-Director, Center for Racial Justice and Criminal Justice Reform, University of Arkansas at Little Rock William H. Bowen School of Law. J.D., Howard University School of Law. This article was prepared for presentation at "The Evolution of Street Knowledge: Hip Hop's Influence on Law and Culture" a symposium held at the West Virginia University College of Law on February 12-43, 2009. Proceedings can be viewed at http://law.wvu.edu/streetknowledge. I am deeply appreciative to Cathie Montes, Utah Supreme Court, for amazing administrative support and transcription assistance at the very early drafting stages of this piece. For terrific research assistance, I am grateful to Kim Matras, West Virginia University College of Law, class of 2009. For providing critical feedback, I am grateful to Lavinia Mann Cummings and Jo Davies. For reading and commenting on various versions of this article, I am grateful to Professor D. Aaron Lacy, Southern Methodist University Dedman School of Law and Professor Anne Marie Lofaso, West Virginia University College of Law. For exceptional editing insights and professionalism, I am grateful to the Santa Clara Law Review staff and in particular its executive leadership. This article draws extensively from the writings of Professor Paul Butler, George Washington University Law School, and I respectfully acknowledge his influential role in leading a legal academic exploration of hip-hop and its legitimately important place in legal thought and process. A shorter version of this article appears in the book *The Arts of Imprisonment: Control, Resistance and Empowerment* (Ashgate Publishing 2010). Of course, as usual, the politics and errata of this article belong exclusively to me.
2 *See infra* Part IV.
3 *See* Bakari Kitwana, *The Hip Hop generation: Young Blacks and the crisis in African American Culture* 4 (2002) (defining the hip-hop generation as "those young African Americans born between 1965 and 1984 who came of age in the [1980s] and [1990s]) and who share a specific set of values and attitudes"). Kitwana further states: "At the core are our thoughts about family, relationships, child rearing, career, racial identity, race relations, and politics. Collectively, these views make up a complex worldview that has not been concretely defined." *Id.; see also* Paul Butler, Much respect: Toward a Hip-Hop theory of punishment. *Stanford Law Review*, 56, 983, 986–987 (2004) ("The hip-hop nation is gaining political power, and seems more inclined to use it than has historically been the case with youth or artists.").
4 Butler, *supra* note 2, at 997; *see also* Paul Butler, Let's Get Free: A Hip-Hop Theory of Justice (2009).
5 *See* Butler, *supra* note 2, at 985.
6 *See id.*
7 *See infra* Parts III, IV.

8 *See infra* Part IV.
9 *See infra* Part N.A.
10 *See infra* Parts
11 *See infra* Part IV.
12 *See infra* Part N.C.
13 *See And You Don't Stop: 30 Years of Hip-Hop, Episode 1, Back in the Day* (VH-1 television broadcast June 2005) ("These young kids came from poverty and desolation and conquered the world." (quoting Bill Adler, Def Jam Records, 1984–1990)); *see also* Andre L. Smith, Other people's property: Hip-Hop's inherent clashes with property laws and its ascendance as global counter culture. *Virginia Sports and Entertainment Law Journal, 7,* 59, 68 (2007) ("Globally, hip-hop art and culture have been adopted by poor youths around the world, who rely on hip-hop to express their visions of the future and frustrations with the present." (citing Tricia Rose, Black Noise: RAP Music and Black Culture in Contemporary America 19 (1994))).
14 *See* Press Release, Nielsen Soundscan, 2008 U.S. Music Purchases Exceed 1.5 Billion; Growth in Overall Music Purchases Exceeds 10% (Dec. 31, 2008), http://www.businesswire.com/portal/site/home/permalink/?ndmViewId= news_view&newsId=20081231005304&newsLang=en (describing top ten album sales in 2008 where *Tha Carter III,* by Lil' Wayne ranks first; *Paper Trail,* by T.I. ranks eighth; and *I Am... Sasha Fierce,* by Beyonce ranks tenth); *see also* Smith, *supra* note 12, at 66–67 (citing Jeff Chang, *Can't Stop Won't Stop: A History of the Hip-Hop Generation* 418 (2005)) ("Music industry executives began signing talent from other continents, such as Africa and Europe."); *id.* at 60 ("[Y]oung Palestinian and Brazilian youths have embraced hip-hop as their way of expressing dissatisfaction with their social order").
15 *See* Press Release, Nielsen Soundscan, *supra* note 13.
16 *See* Lynette Holloway, The angry appeal of eminem is cutting across racial lines. *The New York Times,* Oct. 28, 2002, at C1, *available at* http://query.nytimes. com/gst/fullpage.html?res=9B02E 5D6163FF93BA15753C 1 A9649C8B63&sec=&spon=&pagewanted=1 ("Hip-hop artists are a proven box-office draw. 'Barbershop,' an urban comedy starring Ice Cube, grossed an estimated $69.5 million by Saturday since its release on [September] 13. 'Brown Sugar,' a hip-hop love story starring Taye Diggs, grossed $22.4 million since its release on [October] 11. Last year, 'Exit Wounds,' starring DMX, grossed $52 million."); *see also* NOTORIOUS (Fox Searchlight 2009); Hustle & Flow (Paramount Classics MTV Films 2005); 8 Mile (Universal Studios and Dreamworks 2002); Belly (Artisan Entertainment 1998); Menace II Society (New Line Cinema 1993); Boyz-n-the-Hood (Columbia Pictures 1992); Juice (Paramount Pictures 1992); Krush Groove (Warner Bros 1985).
17 *See* Jane Ivory, *Forbes Names Jay-Z Richest Rap Mogul,* EFLUXMEDIA, Aug. 17, 2007, http://www.efluxmedia.com/news_Forbes_Names_Jay_Z_Richest _Rap_ Mogul_07806.html (discussing Jay-Z as the current president and CEO of Def Jam and Roc-A-Fella Records and examining other artists such as Diddy, Eminem, and Timbaland as business entrepreneurs).
18 *See* Wendy Kale, Common: "If I Had to Choose, Making Movies Would Win." *Colorado Daily,* Feb. 19, 2009, http://www.coloradodaily.com/ci_12956569?IADID=Search-www.coloradodaily.com-www.coloradodaily.com (describing how

hip-hop artist Common made his transition into motion pictures in the 2007 film *Smokin' Aces* and also appeared in the action film *Wanted); see also* The Internet Movie Database, Mos Def, http://wwvv.imdb.com/name/nm0080049/ (last visited Feb. 25, 2009) (indicating that Mos Def has appeared in such major motion pictures as *16 Blocks, Brown Sugar,* and *The Italian Job);* The Internet Movie Database, Queen Latifah, http://www.imdb.com/name/nm0001451/ (last visited Feb. 25, 2009) (listing the number of major motion pictures in which Queen Latifah has starred, including *Chicago, The Secret Life of Bees,* and *Set It Off); The New York Times,* Times Topics: Ludacris, http://topics.nytimes.com/top/reference/timestopics/peopleMudacris/index.html? scp=1&sq=ludacris%20turned%20actor&st=cse (last visited Feb. 22, 2009) ("His acting career has grown with roles in 'Crash,' 'RocknRolla' and 'Max Payne,' in which he uses his real name, Chris Bridges.").

19 *See* Jeffrey McKinney, *Rags to Riches: Hip-Hop Moguls Use Groundbreaking Designs and Star Power to Challenge Major Clothing Labels and Become a Force in the $164 Billion Fashion Industry—The Hip-Hop Economy: Part 4 of a Series,* BLACK ENTERPRISE, Sept. 2002, http://findarticles.com/p/articles/mi_m1365/is_2_33/ai_91040610/ (stating that Sean Combs, better known as P. Diddy, has his own successful clothing line, "Sean John," while hip-hop artist Jay-Z also has a clothing line, "Rocawear").

20 *See* Natalie Finn, *Snoop Dogg Gets Real,* E! ONLINE, July 13, 2007, http://www.eonline.com/uberblog/b55631_Snoop_Dogg_Gets_Real.html (stating that Snoop Dogg signed on to star in a reality series on E!); *see also* Run's House, http://www.mtv.com/ontv/dyn/runs_house/series.jhtml (last visited Feb. 22, 2009) (stating that Reverend Run, from the hip-hop group Run DMC, stars in his own reality show on MTV titled, "Run's House"); BET.com, Tiny & Toya, http://www.bet.com/ontv/betshows/tinyandtoya/ (last visited July 17, 2009) (featuring in a reality television program Tameka "Tiny" Cottle and Antonia "Toya" Carter, the girlfriend/wife of T.I. and the ex-wife of Lil Wayne—Wayne Carter—respectively). The Hip Hop Law blog reveals:

> We get a glimpse inside hip hop star T.I.'s mansion as his girlfriend, who is now rumored to be his wife, capitalizes on his incarceration. Tameka "Tiny" Cottle, a former member of the 90s hip hop soul female singing group Xscape, is talented in her own right, but for the most part was forgotten. With renewed media interest in all of the "T.I. goes to jail" hoopla, Tiny is back in the spotlight. Antonia "Toya" Carter, the ex-wife of Wayne Carter a.k.a. superstar rapper Lil' Wayne, uncovers the unknown side of the musician's family.

Posting of Kamille Wolff to Hip Hop Law.com, http://hiphoplaw.blogspot.com/2009/07/tnt-tiny-n-toya-are-dynamite.html (July 14, 2009).

21 *See* RollingStone, Timbaland Biography, http://www.rollingstone.com/ artists/timbaland/biography (last visited Feb. 22, 2009) (demonstrating that Timbaland is well known for his many successful collaborations, including his work on hip-hop artist Genuine's album, *The Bachelor,* and Nelly Furtado's album, *Loose); see also* Posting of Daniel Kreps, Justin Timberlake, T.I. Team Up for "If I" to Rolling Stone, http://www.rollingstone.com/rockdaily/index.php/ 2008/12/17/justin-timberlake-ti-team-up-for-if-i (Dec. 17, 2008, 15:05 EST).

22 *See* The Hiphop Archive, Hiphop Courses, http://www.hiphoparchive.org/university/courses (last visited Mar.1, 2009) (listing hundreds of hip-hop-based courses offered in upper-level academia through 2009).

23 *See* Butler, *supra* note 3; *see also* D.J. Kool Herc, *Introduction* to Chang, *supra* note 13, at xi; Nelson George, Hip Hop America (Penguin Books 1999) (1998); Bakari Kitwana, Why white kids love Hip-Hop: Wankstas, wiggers, wannabes, and the new reality of race in America (2006); Imani Perry, Prophets of the Hood: Politics and Poetics in Hip Hop (2004); S. Craig Watkins, Hip-Hop matters: Politics, pop culture, and the struggle for the soul of a movement (2005); Horace E. Anderson, Jr., *"Criminal Minded?": Mixtape DJs, the piracy paradox, and lessons for the recording industry. Tennessee Law Review*, 76, 111 (2008); Olufunmilayo B. Arewa, *From J.C. Bach to Hip Hop: Musical borrowing, copyright and cultural context.* North Carolina Law Review, *84*, 547 (2006); Ronald D. Brown, The politics of "Mo' Money, Mo' Money" and the strange dialectic of Hip Hop. *Vanderbilt Journal of Entertainment Law & Practice*, 5, 59 (2003); Akilah N. Folami, *From Habermas to "Get Rich or Die Tryin'": Hip Hop, the Telecommunications Act of 1996, and the Black Public Sphere. The Michigan Journal of Race & Law*, 12, 235 (2007); Brian Goldman, Putting Lamborghini doors on the Escalade: A legal analysis of the unauthorized use of brand names in Rap I Hip-Hop, 8 *Texas Review of Entertainment & Sports Law* 1 (2007); Josh Norek, "You Can't Sing Without the Bling": The toll of excessive sample license fees on creativity in Hip-Hop music and the need for a compulsory sound recording sample license system. *UCLA Entertainment Law Review*, *11*, 83 (2004); Sean-Patrick Wilson, Rap Sheets: The constitutional and societal complications arising from the use of rap lyrics as evidence at criminal trials. *UCLA Entertainment Law Review*, *12*, 345 (2005).

24 *See* Folami, *supra* note 22, at 253 ("Despite its commercial successes and commodification, gangsta rap must continue to be contextualized within its hip hop origins, as it still *gives* voice to what would otherwise be an invisible and marginalized group of Black and Latino male youth."); *see also* M.K. Asante JR., It's bigger than Hip Hop: The rise of the Post-Hip-Hop generation (2008); Chang, *supra* note 13, at xii ("Hip-hop is the voice of this generation. Even if you didn't grow up in the Bronx in the 1970s, hip-hop is there for you. It has become a powerful force. Hip-hop binds all of these people, all of these nationalities, all over the world together.").

25 *See* Rachel E. Sullivan, Rap and race: It's got a nice beat, but what about the message?. *Journal of Black Studies*, *33* 605, 606 (2003) ("By the late 1980s, rap was no longer viewed as a fad but as a distinctive musical form."); Live Leak.com, History of Rap/Hip Hop Music, http://www.liveleak.com/view?i= 909_1221000257 (last visited Feb. 27, 2009).

26 *See* Glenn Collins, Rap music, brash and swaggering, enters mainstream. *The New York Times*, Aug. 29, 1988, at C15, *available at* http://query.nytimes.com/gst/fullpage.html?res=940DE1DF163EF93AA1575BC0A96E948260&sec=&spon=&pagewanted=2. In 1988, the New York Times reported:

> Hip-hop, as the culture of rap is called, originated among young blacks in the Bronx in the 1970s. Instead of fading like many previous fads, rap's energy has become increasingly irresistible to an international audience

of teenagers and pre-teenagers. As in other subcultural trends that have matured into mass phenomena, rap language and style are entering older, more racially diverse, middle-class and suburban communities.

Hip-hop words from what was once an underclass subculture are now common parlance among America's youth.

"The mainstream always hoped it would be a fad that would die," Mr. Bambaataa said. But instead, he maintained, the distinctive hip-hop vocabulary, clothes and culture has been important in empowering and giving status to an impoverished and isolated generation of urban young people that society found threatening.

27 *Id.*
See *id.* ("Like early rock-and-roll, rap's tough sound and aggressive esthetic can be abrasive and anti-authoritarian, raising concern among some parents and critics about hip-hop's sexual explicitness, macho swaggering and association with violence 'The cultural police are always threatened by new movements, and greet them unfailingly with hysteria... ").

28 See *id.*; see also Encyclopedia Britannica's Guide to Black History, Hip-Hop, http://www.britannica.com/blackhistory/article-9117537 (last visited Feb. 26, 2009) (discussing hip-hop as a "cultural movement" and examining the evolution of "gangsta rap" and its beginnings). Britannica's Guide to Black History states:

The most significant response to New York hip-hop, though, came from Los Angeles, beginning in 1989 with N.W.A.'s dynamic album *Straight Outta Compton*. N.W.A. (N****z With Attitude) and former members of that group—Ice Cube, Eazy E, and producer Dr. Dre—led the way as West Coast rap grew in prominence in the early 1990s. Their graphic, frequently violent tales of real life in the inner city, as well as those of Los Angeles rappers such as Ice-T (remembered for his 1992 single *Cop Killer*) and Snoop Doggy Dogg and of East Coast counterparts such as Schoolly D, gave rise to the genre known as gangsta rap.

Id.; Public Enemy, It Takes a Nation of Millions to Hold Us Back (Def Jam Records 1988); Public Enemy, Fear of a Black Planet (Def Jam Records 1990); N.W.A., Straight Outta Compton (Ruthless Records 1988); Boogie Down Productions, Criminal Minded (B-Boy Records 1987); Boogie Down Productions, By All Means Necessary (Jive Records 1988); ICE T., *6 in the Morning, on* Dog 'N the Wax (Ya Don't Quit-Part II) (Techno Hop Records 1986); ICE T., *Cop Killer, on* Body Count (Sire/Warner Bros. Records 1992).

29 *See infra* notes 31–34; *see also* Butler, *supra* note 2, at 992 ("Market studies indicate that about 75 % of people who buy hip-hop music are non-black."); Bakari Kitwana, *The Cotton Club: Black-Conscious Hip-Hop deals with an overwhelmingly white live audience,* VILLAGE VOICE, June 21, 2005, http://www.villagevoice.com/2005-06-21/music/the-cotton-club ("Whites run hip-hop, they say, from the business executives at major labels to the suburban teen consumers. But the often-intoned statistic claiming that [seventy] percent of American hip-hop sells to white people may cover up more than it reveals.").

30 *See* Smith, *supra* note 12, at 69.
31 *Id.*
32 *See* NME.com, NWA Biography, http://www.nme.com/artists/nwa (last visited Mar. 17, 2009) ("In 1989, the FBI investigated Straight Outta Compton's infamous 'Fuck Tha Police' It set a precedent for numerous actions against N.W.A., including the first time anyone in the music industry had received a threatening letter from the FBI."); *see also* N.W.A. *Outta Compton in 1989: 50 Moments that Changed the History of Rock & Roll,* Rolling Stone, June 24, 2004, http://www.rollingstone.com/artists/nwa/articles/story/6085509/nwa_outta compton_in_1989 ("N.W.A—N****z With Attitude—put Los Angeles on the hip-hop map by combining funk rhythms with staccato rhymes that condemned racist cops and offered a nihilistic chronicle of drug dealing, casual street violence and crack ho's The FBI sent a letter to N.W.A's record company, Priority, six months after the album's release, accusing the label of selling a record that encouraged violence against law enforcement.").
33 *See* James LeMoyne, *Limelight nothing new for Sheriff in Rap Case. New York Times,* June 26, 1990, at A12, *available at* http://query.nytimes.com/gst/fullpage.html?res=9C0CE5D81638F935A15755C0A966958260&n.Top%2FReference%2FTimes%20Topics%2FSubjects%2FP%2FPornography%20and%200bscenity (discussing Broward County Sheriff Nick Navarro's "successful effort to have 2 Live Crew's sexually explicit record album 'As Nasty as They Wanna Be' declared the first legally obscene record in America"); *see also* The Internet Movie Database, Ice-T—Biography, http://ww-w.imdb.com/name/nm0001384/bio (last visited Mar. 2, 2009) ("[Ice-T's] most infamous song, the heavy metal 'Cop Killer,' was one of the major battle [s] in the cultural wars of the 1990s, in which cultural conservatives enlisted the Moses of the right wing, Charlton Heston, to get Ice-T dropped from his then-label, Sire/Warner Bros.").
34 *See* Emmett G. Price III, Hip Hop Culture 74–75 (2006) (discussing the Tipper Gore-led formation of Parents' Music Resource Center and its goal of banning explicit material on recordings in rap, rock, and heavy metal music and the RIAA's introduction of a uniform labeling system for records with explicit content reading "Parental Advisory—Explicit Lyrics").
35 *See* Russell A. Potter, Spectacular Vernaculars: HIP-Hop And The Politics of Postmodernism 95 (1995) ("In 1994, the reaction against this particular genre reached a crisis point in the form of congressional hearings instigated by Dr. C. Delores Tucker. Dr. Tucker... took offense to 'gangsta rap' lyrics, and organized a series of protests in the Washington, D.C. area Unlike Tipper Gore and her dormant Parents' Music Resource Center, Tucker wanted more than warning labels; she demanded an outright ban on 'gangsta' rap records.").
36 *See* Kitwana, *supra* note 2, at 4 (defining the hip-hop generation); *see also* Butler, *supra* note 2, at 986 (discussing the "hip-hop nation").
37 *See* Christian D. Rutherford, Note, "Gangsta" Culture in a policed state: The crisis in legal ethics formation amongst hip-hop youth. National BLACK L.J., *18,* 305 (2004–2005).
38 *See* Shaheem Reid, *Barack Obama and Hip-Hop: Does the Support of Jay-Z, Nas, T.I. Hurt His Chances?,* MTV.COM, Aug. 20, 2008, http://www.mtv.com/news/articles/1593139/20080819/jay_z.jhtml;*see also* Aliya Ewing, *Obama Addresses Hip Hop; Meets with Jay-Z and Kanye West,* HIP HOP DX, Jan.10,2008, http://www.

hiphopdx.com/index/news/id.6204/title.barack-obama-addresses-hip-hop-meets-with-jay-z-and-kanye-west ("With the primaries in full swing, the voice of young Black America and the Hip Hop vote will continue to be a focal point in the media. So far, rappers including Common, Rhymefest and Talib Kweli have voiced their support for Obama."); William Kristol, Generation Obama? Perhaps Not. *The New York Times*, Mar. 17, 2008, at A19, *available at*http://www.nytimes.com/2008/03/17/opinion/17kristol.html (referring to "Generation Obama," as a "grass-roots movement led by young activists with a simple goal: electing Barack Obama the next president of the United States of America"); Azi Paybarah, Obama's Hip-Hop admirers. *The New York Observer*, Mar. 4, 2008, http://www.observer.com/2008/obama-s-hip-hop-admirers ("If Barack Obama is the Democratic nominee, it's a pretty safe assumption that he's going to have overwhelming support from the hip-hop community.").

39 *See* Talib Kweli, Keynote Address at West Virginia University College of Law Symposium, The Evolution of Street Knowledge: Hip Hop's Influence on Law and Culture (Feb. 12, 2009), http://lawmediasite.wvu.edu/mediasite/ Viewer/?peid=59733166612c4b28aa405284c2b22e99. During live remarks made at West Virginia University College of Law's symposium, keynote speaker Kweli refers to President Obama as the "hip hop President." *Id.; see also* Imani Cheers & Crystal Holmes, The Audacity of Hip-Hop. *NEWSWEEK*, Sept. 25, 2008, http://www.newsweek.com/id/160832.

40 *See NPR Weekend Edition: Obama Hip-Hop: From Mixtapes to Mainstream* (NPR radio broadcast Nov. 9, 2008), http://www.npr.org/templates/ story/story.php?storyld=96748462. NPR reported that President Obama recognized the support from the hip-hop generation:

> "The challenge that Barack Obama had was really to be able to wink to the hip-hop community and say, 'I really can't acknowledge you in the mainstream, but understand that I'm hearing what your critique is, I'm hearing what your concerns are, and you now have a wide-open space in the so-called underground... to talk about why my candidacy is important,'" [Professor Mark Anthony] Neal says. "And I think many of the rappers, particularly the very visible mainstream rappers, understood that strategy, because it's a strategy that they employ all the time, also. There's a version of, for instance, Snoop Dogg that sells records, but that's a very different version of Snoop Dogg that's sitting with Larry King talking about the election."
> *Id.*

41 Dr. Cornel West, Professor, Princeton Univ., Keynote Address at the West Virginia University College of Law Symposium, The Evolution of Street Knowledge: Hip Hop's Influence on Law and Culture (Feb. 13, 2009) (transcript on file with author) (describing hip-hop "at its best" as a movement that inspires and affects listeners based on its authenticity and willingness to deal with the reality of pain, inequality, and disappointment in life, when most Americans avoid dealing with difficult issues of racism, sexism inequality, poverty, and powerlessness).

42 *See And You Don't Stop, supra* note 12 (featuring an interview with Ice-T).

43 *See* Symposium, The Evolution of Street Knowledge: Hip Hop's Influence on Law and Culture(Feb.12-13, 2009).The webstreams from day one and two can be found at Law Mediasite Catalog, http://lawmediasite.wvu.edu/mediasite/catalog, with many symposium panelists making references to the distinction between socially conscious hip-hop and gangsta rap, including Professors Pamela Bridgewater, Kamille Wolff, andré douglas pond cummings, Horace Anderson, and Akilah Folami.

44 *See* Butler, *supra* note 2, at 991 (citing the Washington Post describing "two faces of hip-hop," distinguishing between the "conscious" side of hip-hop and the "bling-bling" or "gangsta" rap); *see also* Rutherford, *supra* note 36, at 322. Rutherford states that a distinction exists between socially conscious hip-hop artists and more negative hip-hop, and opines without citing support:

> There are plenty of artists recording Hip-Hop music today who do not espouse violence: Common, Talib Kweli and the Roots, to name a few. But the level of attention, exposure, and airplay that these artists receive pales in comparison to their platinum-selling counterparts, all of whom choose to infuse their albums in varying degrees, with anti-social content.
> *Id*.

45 *See, e.g.,* Slick Rick, *Children's Story, on* The Great Adventures of Slick Rick (Def Jam/Columbia 1988); *see also* Tupac Shakur, *Changes, on* Greatest Hits (Death Row Records 1998). *But see* Slick Rick, *Treat Her Like a Prostitute, on* The Great Adventures of Slick Rick (Def Jaro/Columbia1988); Tupac Shakur, *I Get Around, on* Strictly 4 MY N.I.G.G.A.Z. (Interscope 1993).

46 *See* Pamela Bridgewater, Professor of Law, American University Washington College of Law, Stepping to the Mic: Hip Hop's Expanding Voice in Social and Political Discourse, Address at the West Virginia University College of Law Symposium, The Evolution of Street Knowledge: Hip Hop's Influence on Law and Culture (Feb. 13, 2009), http://lawmediasite.wvu.edu/mediasite/ Viewer/ ?peid=0f77bcf641b64295acde0a810e573f97.

47 KRS-ONE, Edutainment (Jive/RCA Records 1990).

48 Public Enemy, *Fight the Power, on* Do The Right Thing—SOUNDTRACK (Tamla 1989); *see also* Public Enemy, *Fight the Power, on* Fear of a Black Planet (Def Jam/Columbia Records 1990); YouTube.com, Public Enemy Fight the Power, http://www.youtube.com/watch?v=M_t13-OJoyc (last visited Oct. 13, 2009).

49 *See And You Don't Stop, supra* note 12 (featuring an interview with Tupac Shakur).

50 *See id.* (featuring an interview with Ice-T).

51 *See* Smith, *supra* note 12, at 60.

52 Lil' Wayne, *Don't Get It, on* Tha Carter III (Cash Money Records/Universal Records/Young Money Entertainment 2008).

53 *See infra* note 63 and accompanying text.

54 *See infra* notes 64, 66 and accompanying text.

55 N.W.A., *Fuck Tha Police, on* Straight Outta Compton (Ruthless Records/Priority Records 1988).

56 *See generally* andré douglas pond cummings, Just another gang: "When the cops are crooks who can you trust?." *Howard Law Journal, 41,* 383 (1998) (describing the "siege mentality" that permeates most large, urban police departments and

discussing the "War on Drugs" as a war on small scale, inner city drug dealers rather than a war against the source countries and cartels).

57 The term "soft crime" is typically understood to include "non-violent drug offenses." See Bruce Shapiro, *Hard Time For Soft Crimes*, SALON.COM, July 31, 2000, http://archive.salon.com/news/feature/2000/07/31/drugs/index.html ("'Poor Prescription: The Costs of Imprisoning Drug Offenders in the United States,' published by the Justice Policy Institute, reveals in stark terms the consequences of the bipartisan, two-decade love affair with mandatory sentences and harsh drug policies. The nation's prison population now stands at [two] million, but according to the report, this has less to do with making streets safer than with locking up nonviolent drug users.").

58 *See supra* notes 31–34; *see also* Robert Levine, Film; The thawing of ice cube. *The New York* Times, Feb.1, 2004, §2, at 13, *available at* http://query.nytimes.com/gst/fullpage.html?res=9A00E3D81538F932A35751C0 A9629C8B63&scp=2&sq=fbi%20letter%20to%20NWA%20record%20label&st=cs e ("N.W.A., which in the late 1980s defined West Coast hip-hop with layered beats and brutal lyrics, probably offended more people before breakfast than most artists do all day; the F.B.I. sent the group's record label a letter expressing its disapproval of the song [Expletive] Tha Police.'"); Jon Pareles, Critic's notebook; Public enemy, loud and angry, is far from its own best friend. *The New York Times*, Dec. 26, 1989, at C15, *available at* http://query.nytimes.com/gst/fullpage.html?res=950DEEDD163EF935A1575 1C1 A96F948260. *The New York Times*, detailing the swirling controversy that always surrounded Public Enemy in the 1990s, reported:

> The rap group Public Enemy has a knack for shooting itself in the foot. Its response to a controversy last summer over anti-Semitic statements by its "minister of information" has now appeared in lyrics from its new single, "Welcome to the Terrordome," that also seem to cross the line into anti-Semitism.
> Public Enemy has been in rap's musical and political vanguard since 1987, when the group revolutionized the sound of rap with its dense, jarring, propulsive sonic collages. The booming voice of Carlton (Chuck D.) Ridenhour quickly became synonymous with a commitment to militant black self-determination.
> *Id.*

59 *See* Pareles, *supra* note 57.
60 *See* Laura Barton, *"Rap is Elitist,"* Guardian (UK), May 7, 2003, http://www.guardian.co.uk/music./2003/may/07/artsfeatures.popandrock ("Chuck D rapped about the problems blighting the black community, and memorably described hip-hop as the black CNN.' ").
61 *NPR Weekend Edition: Obama Hip-Hop: From Mixtapes to Mainstream* (NPR broadcast Nov. 9, 2008), http://www.npr.org/templates/story/story.php?storyId=96748462.
62 Butler, *supra* note 2, at 986.
63 *Id.* at 985.
64 *See* Timothy Egan, War on crack retreats, still taking prisoners. *The New York Times*, Feb. 28, 1999, §1, at 1, *available at* http://query.nytimes.com/gst/fullpage.html?res=-

950CEODC 123CF93BA15751C0A96F958260&sec=&spon=&pagewanted=5 ("In state prisons, blacks make up nearly [sixty] percent of the people serving time on drug offenses, according to Justice Department figures, though they are only [twelve] percent of the general population and [fifteen] percent of regular drug users."); *see also supra* Part III (detailing hip-hop lyrics that discuss the inequities and biases in criminal law and punishment).

65 *See* Butler, *supra* note 2, at 988; *see also* David A. Sklansky, Cocaine, race, and equal protection. *Stanford Law Review, 47,* 1283,1290–1298, 1296(1995) ("[Congress] instituted a mandatory sentence for possession of crack cocaine, but not powder cocaine. The punishment for sellers was especially harsh. To receive the same sentence as a crack distributor, a powder distributor must possess one hundred times the quantity of cocaine."); Egan, *supra* note 63 ("As the war on drugs set up special penalties on crack, however, law enforcement focused on the highly visible, often violent crack trade in city neighborhoods, rather than the larger traffic in cocaine going on behind closed doors across the country. The result: Nearly [ninety] percent of the people locked up for crack under Federal drug laws are black "); *supra* notes 51, 54 and accompanying text; *infra* notes 67–81 (detailing hip-hop lyrics that discuss the inequities and biases in criminal law and punishment).

66 *See Rodney King Testifies About Night of Beating, The New York Times,* Jan. 22, 1993, at A16, *available at*http://query.nytimes.com/gst/fullpageltml?res=9FOCE1D D1039F931A15752C0A965958260(describingRodneyKing's harrowing testimony of the infamous police brutality incident); *see also* cummings, *supra* note 55 (describing the "siege mentality" that infects most metropolitan police forces across the United States); Sewell Chan, The Abner Louima Case, 10 Years Later. *The New York Times,* Aug. 9, 2007, http://cityroom.blogs.nytimes.com/2007/08/09/the-abner-louima-case-10-years-later/?scp=l&sq=,%20Abner%20Louima&st=cse ("Ten years ago today, a [thirty]-year-old Haitian immigrant named Abner Louima was arrested and sodomized with a broomstick inside a restroom in the 70th Precinct station house in Brooklyn. The case became a national symbol of police brutality and fed perceptions that New York City police officers were harassing or abusing young black men as part a citywide crackdown on crime."); Robert D. McFadden, *Police kill man after a queens bachelor party. The New York Times,* Nov. 26, 2006, § 1, at 1, *available at*http://www.nytimes.com/2006/11/26/nyregion/ 26cops. html?scp=8&sq=sean%20bell&st=cse (discussing the death of Sean Bell who was killed when police officers fired fifty rounds of bullets into Bell's car following his bachelor's party the evening before his wedding).

67 *See* Ben Wallace-Wells, How America lost the war on drugs. *Rolling Stone,* Dec. 13, 2007, at 90, *available at*http://www.rollingstone.com/politics/story/17438347/ how_america_lost_the_war_on_drugs/1(detailing the failed efforts of the Reagan era "War on Drugs"); *see also* William J. Stuntz, Unequal justice. *Harvard Law Review,* 121, 1969, 1970 (2008) ("Inequality is a core feature of American criminal justice The effects of both the fall of criminal punishment and its subsequent rise were disproportionately felt in urban black neighborhoods."); John A. Powell & Eileen B. Hershenov, Hostage to the drug war: The national purse, the constitution and the black community. *UC Davis Law Review,* 24, 557, 558–559 (1991) ("[I]t is clear that the war on drugs has not extinguished the drug trade. Rather, the real victims of this war are the minority poor and the Bill of Rights. While the war against

Thug Life: Hip-Hop's Curious Relationship 61

drugs potentially compromises the rights of all Americans, it has a particularly devastating impact upon the recently gained rights of minorities. In fact, the war on drugs could more aptly be called a war on the minority populations.").
68 *See* Grandmaster Flash, *The Message, on* The Message (Sugar Hill Records 1982).

> You grow in the ghetto, living second rate / And your eyes will sing a song of deep hate / The places you play and where you stay / Looks like one great big alley way / You'll admire all the number book takers / Thugs, pimps, and pushers and the big money makers / Driving big cars, spending twenties and tens / And you wanna grow up to be just like them / Smugglers, scramblers, burglars, gamblers / Pickpockets, peddlers and even pan-handlers / You say I'm cool, I'm no fool / But then you wind up dropping out of high school / Now you're unemployed, all null 'n' void / Walking around like you're Pretty Boy Floyd / Turned stickup kid, look what you done did/ Got sent up for a eight year bid ...
> *Id.*

69 *See* Public Enemy, *Fight the Power, on* Do The Right Thing Soundtrack (Motown Records 1988).

> To revolutionize make a change nothin's strange / People, people we are the same / No we're not the same / Cause we don't know the game / What we need is awareness, we can't get careless / You say what is this? / My beloved let's get down to business / Mental self defensive fitness... Fight the Power
> *Id.*

70 *See* Public Enemy, *Don't Believe the Hype, on* It Takes a Nation of Millions to Hold Us Back (Def Jam Records/Columbia Records 1988).

> Turn up the radio / They claim that I'm a criminal / By now I wonder how / Some people never know / The enemy could be their friend, guardian / I'm not a hooligan / I rock the party and / Clear all the madness, I'm not a racist / Preach to teach to all / 'Cause some they never had this

Id.
71 *See* Public Enemy, *Black Steel in the Hour of Chaos, on* It Takes a Nation of Millions to Hold Us Back (Def Jam Records/Columbia Records 1988).

> I got a letter from the government / The other day / I opened and read it / It said they were suckers / They wanted me for their army or whatever / Picture me given' a damn—I said never / Here is a land that never gave a damn / About a brother like me and myself / Because they never did / I wasn't wit' it, but just that very minute... / It occurred to me / The suckers had authority

Id.
72 *See* Public Enemy, *911 is a Joke, on* Fear of a Black Planet (Def Jam Records/Columbia Records 1990) ("911 is a joke we don't want 'em / I call a cab 'cause a cab will come

quicker / The doctors huddle up and call a flea flicker / The reason that I say that 'cause they / Flick you off like fleas / They be laughing at ya while you're crawling on your knees.").

73 *See* N.W.A., *Fuck Tha Police, on* STRAIGHT OUTTA COMPTON (Ruthless Records 1988) ("Fuck the police coming straight from the underground / Young n***a got it bad cuz I'm brown / And not the other color so police think / They have the authority to kill a minority").

74 *See* N.W.A., *100 Miles and Running, on* 100 Miles and Runnin' (Ruthless Records 1990).

> Running like a n***a I hate to lose. / Show me on the news but I hate to be abused; / I know it was a set-up. / So now I'm gonna get up. / Even if the FBI wants me to shut up. / But I've got 10,000 n****s strong. / They got everybody singing my "Fuck Tha Police" song / And while they treat my group like dirt, / Their whole fuck'n family is wearing our T-shirts.

Id.

75 *See* Tupac Shakur, *Brenda's Got a Baby, on* 2PACALYPSE Now (Interscope Records 1991) ("[Clause I bet Brenda doesn't even know / just cause your in tha ghetto doesn't mean you can't grow / but oh, that's a thought, my own revelation / do whatever it takes to resist the temptation.").

76 *See* Tupac Shakur, *Keep Ya Head Up, on* Strictly For My N****Z (Interscope Records 1993).

> And since we all came from a woman / Got our name from a woman and our game from a woman / I wonder why we take from our women / Why we rape our women, do we hate our women? / I think it's time to kill for our women / Time to heal our women, be real to our women.

Id.

77 *See* Tupac Shakur, *To Live & Die in L.A., on* The Don KILLUMINATI: The 7 Day Theory (Death Row Records 1996).

> It's the, City of Angels and constant danger / South Central LA, can't get no stranger / Full of drama like a soap opera, on the curb / Watching the ghetto bird helicopters, I observe / So many n****z getting three strikes, tossed in jail/ I swear the pen the right across from hell, I can't cry / Cause it's on now, I'm just a n***a on his own now.

Id.

78 Ice Cube, AMERIKKKAS Most Wanted (Priority 1990).
79 *See* Ice Cube, *Endangered Species (Tales from the Darkside), on* AMERIKKKAS Most Wanted (Priority Records 1990).

> Every cop killer goes ignored / They just send another n***a to the morgue / A point scored—they could give a fuck about us / They rather catch us with guns and white powder / If I was old, they'd probably be a friend of me / Since I'm young, they consider me the enemy / They kill ten of me to get the job correct / To serve, protect, and break a n****s neck.

Id.
80 *See* Ice Cube, *Dead Homiez, on* Kill at Will (Priority Records 1990).

> Another homie got murdered on a shakedown... / And his mother is at the funeral, havin' a nervous breakdown / Two shots hit him in the face when they blasted... / A framed picture and a closed casket / A single file line about 50 cars long / All drivin' slow with they lights on / He got a lot of flowers and a big wreath / What good is that when you're six feet deep? / I look at that shit and gotta think to myself / And thank God for my health / 'Cause nobody really ever know / When it's gonna be they family on the front row / So I take everything slow, go with the flow / And shut my motherfuckin' mouth if I don't know... / 'Cause that's what Pops told me / But I wish he could have said it... to my dead homiez.

Id.
81 Boogie Down Productions, Edutainment (Jive/RCA Records 1990).
82 *See* Boogie Down Productions, *Love's Gonna Get'cha (Material Love), on* Edutainment (Jive/RCA Records 1990).

> But there's no dollars for nothing else / I got beans, rice, and bread on my shelf / Every day I see my mother struggling / Now it's time, I've got to do something / I look for work I get dissed like a jerk / I do odd jobs and come home like a slob / So here comes Rob [drug dealer], his gold is shimmery / He gives me two hundred for a quick delivery / I do it once, I do it twice / Now there's steak with the beans and rice / My mother's nervous but she knows the deal / My sister's gear now has sex appeal / My brother's my partner and we're getting paper / Three months later we run our own caper / My family's happy everything is new / Now tell me what the fuck am I supposed to do? / That's why / [Chorus:] Love's gonna get you / Love's gonna get you... / You fall in love with your chain / You fall in love with your car / Love's gonna sneak right up and snuff you from behind / So I want you to check the story out as we go down the line.

Id.
83 *See supra* note 65; *see also* Common, Finding Forever (G.O.O.D. Music/Geffen 2007); Immortal Technique, Revolutionary Vol. 1 (Viper Records 2005); Mos DEF, Black on Both Sides (Rawkus Records 1999); Talib Kweli, The Beautiful Struggle (Rawkus Records 2004).
84 *See* Joycelyn M. Pollock, Prisons: Today and Tomorrow 9–10 (2d ed. 1997); *see also* Rutherford, *supra* note 36, at 305 ("Legal scholars have long proffered the idea that the criminal law is effective, and justified, in part, *because* of its deterrent effects. The common notion is that punishment rendered by the criminal legal system, as well as the moral condemnation and stigma associated with a criminal record, will serve to counter-act the compulsion individuals have to commit anti-social behavior.").
85 *See* Pollock, *supra* note 83, at 9–10.
86 *See id.*
87 *See id.*
88 *See* Butler, *supra* note 2, at 1000.

89 *See* Reginald Leamon Robinson, Race, myth and narrative in the social construction of the Black Self. *How. Law Journal*, 40, 1, 7 (1996) ("Today, few law professors are willing to acknowledge that a white male perspective has shaped legal academe in a manner which stills invades, wounds, and destroys their colleagues of color."); *see also* andré douglas pond cummings, Grutter v. Bollinger, Clarence Thomas, Affirmative action and the treachery of originalism: "The sun don't shine here in this part of town." *Harvard BlackLetter Law Journal*, 21 1 (2005).

90 *See generally* Cummings, *supra* note 88; Michele H. Kalstein et al., Calculating injustice: The fixation of punishment as crime control. *The Harvard Civil Rights – Civil Liberties Law Review*, 27, 575, 588 & n. 52 (1992) ("'We the people' is misleading because it claims to speak for everyone when it is actually the voice of 'a political faction trying to constitute itself as a unit of many disparate voices; its power lasts only as long as the contradictory voices remain silenced.'" (quoting Angela P. Harris, *Race and essentialism in feminist legal theory. The Stanford Law Review*, 42, 581, 583 (1990))); Robinson, *supra* note 88. The authors state that utilitarian thinking "enables those in power to create 'apparently neutral and universal rules which in effect burden or exclude anyone who does not share the characteristics of privileged, white, Christian, able-bodied, heterosexual, adult men for whom those rules were actually written.'" *Id.* (quoting Martha Minow & Elizabeth V. Spelman, Symposium on the renaissance of pragmatism in American legal thought. *Southern California Law Review*, 63, 1597, 1601 (1990)).

91 *See* Butler, *supra* note 2, at 1000-01.

92 *Id. at* 1000 (footnote omitted).

93 *See generally* Dr. Cornel West, Professor, Princeton Univ., Keynote Address at the West Virginia University College of Law Symposium, The Evolution of Street Knowledge: Hip Hop's Influence on Law and Culture (Feb. 13, 2009) (transcript on file with author) (discussing frankly the inequities in the criminal justice system and the need for rehabilitative principles in punishment regimes, particularly for soft drug crime offenders).

94 *See* Larry E. Walker, Law and more disorder! The disparate impact of federal mandatory sentencing for drug related offenses on the Black Community. *Journal of Suffolk Acad. Law*, 10, 97, 119 (1995) ("The majority of the arrests made are of young black males who are addicted to and in possession of small quantities of drugs or who are low-level distributors. The facts seem to indicate that the war on drugs can easily be perceived as a war on the black community."); *see also id.* at 98 ("While blacks makeup approximately [twelve] percent of the United States population, over [eighty] percent of all of those arrested for drug related offenses are black." (citing Powell & Hershenov, *supra* note 66, at 568)).

95 *See* Walker, *supra* note 93; *see also* Michael A. Simons, Departing ways: Uniformity, Disparity and Cooperation in Federal Drug Sentences. *Villanova Law Review*, 47, 921, 930 (2002) (discussing the drug sentencing guidelines and mandatory minimum sentences of five years for distributing five grams of crack compared to distributing 500 grams of cocaine); Sklansky, *supra* note 64 (discussing the differences in sentencing for crack cocaine and powder cocaine as a constitutional violation of the Equal Protection Clause).

96 *See* Chuck Colson & Pat Nolan, Prescription for safer communities. *Notre Dame Journal of Law, Ethics & Public Policy*, 18, 387, 389 (2004) ("Offenders are often

sentenced for years to overcrowded prisons where they are exposed to the horrors of violence including homosexual rape, isolation from family and friends, and despair. Instead of working on the outside to repay their victims and support their families, many non-dangerous offenders are idle in prison. Prisons are, indeed, graduate schools of crime.").

97 *See supra* Parts III, IV.A.
98 JAY-Z, A *Ballad for the Fallen Soldier, on* The Blueprint 2: The Gift & The Curse (Def Jam/Island Def Jam 2002); *see also* MetroLyrics.com, Jay-Z—A Ballad for the Fallen Soldier, http://www.metrolyrics.com/a-ballad-for-the-fallen-soldier-lyrics-jayz.html (last visited Sept. 5, 2009).
99 Ludacris Feat. Beanie Sigel, *Do Your Time, on* Release Therapy (Def Jam South/Disturbing Tha Peace 2006); *see also* MetroLyrics.com, Ludacris—Do Your Time Lyrics, http://www.metrolyrics.com/do-your-time-lyrics-ludacris.html (last visited Mar. 4, 2009).
100 T.I., *You Ain't Missin Nothin, on* Paper Trail (Grand Hustle/Atlantic 2008); *see also* MetroLyrics.com, T.I.—You Ain't Missin Nothin Lyrics, http://www.metrolyrics.com/you-aint-missin-nothin-lyrics-ti.html (last visited Mar. 4, 2009).
101 *See* Butler, *supra* note 2, at 998.
102 *Id.*
103 Rutherford, *supra* note 36, at 305.
104 *See generally* Butler, *supra* note 3.
105 *See* Butler, *supra* note 2, at 1002.
106 *See id.*
107 *Id.* at 1004-05.
108 *See id. at* 1001.
109 *See* andré douglas pond cummings, What's race got to do with post-racialism?: Post-Racialism and the financial market meltdown (Jan. 9, 2009) (AALS Annual Meeting Hot Topics Panel Presentation) (unpublished manuscript, on file with author).
110 *See* Butler, *supra* note 3.
111 *See* Smith, *supra* note 12, at 69.
112 *See* Carla Pratt, Professor of Law, Texas Wesleyan School of Law, From the Corner to the Corner Office: Hip Hop's Impact on Corporate Culture and Law, Address at the West Virginia University College of Law Symposium, The Evolution of Street Knowledge: Hip Hop's Influence on Law and Culture (Feb. 13, 2009), http://lawmediasite.wvu.edu/mediasite/catalog.
113 Dr. Cornel West, Professor, Princeton Univ., Keynote Address at the West Virginia University College of Law Symposium, The Evolution of Street Knowledge: Hip Hop's Influence on Law and Culture (Feb. 13, 2009) (transcript on file with author).
114 *See* Folami, *supra* note 22.
115 *See* Anderson, *supra* note 22.
116 Perry, *supra* note 22.
117 *See* Anthony Farley, James C. Matthews Distinguished Professor of Jurisprudence, Albany Law School, Stepping to the Mic: Hip Hop's Expanding Voice in Social and Political Discourse, Address at the West Virginia University College of Law Symposium, The Evolution of Street Knowledge: Hip Hop's Influence on Law

and Culture (Feb. 13, 2009), http://lawmediasite.wvu.edu/ mediasite/Viewer/ ?peid=0f77bcf641b64295acde0a810e573f97.

118 *See Tavis Smiley's State of the Black Union* (C-SPAN television broadcast Feb. 28, 2009) (showing elected representatives discussing the budget crises faced by many states, where legislators cut spending on education and raise spending on prison construction).

Música y Libertad

Victor Mendoza

Introduction

The question of what came first, music or language, create fertile fields for study through biology and evolution of music (biomusicology) and language (biolinguistics) "both for understanding music itself and for a deeper understanding of other aspects of complex, biologically based, but culturally contingent human cognition" (Fitch, 2005, p. 45). According to Merker (2000) even the term music is not universal in humanity, the Greek origin of *music*, (mousiké) includes melody, dance, and poetry (a common denominator in pulse-based rhythmicity), and is closer to tribal concepts that included dance, likening it to modern hip-hop culture. "Musick has Charms to sooth a savage Breast, To soften Rocks, or bend a knotted Oak," (Martin, 2020, n.p.) lines from "The Mourning Bride," a poem by William Congreve in 1697, is commonly misunderstood as "music has charms to soothe a savage beast" (Martin, 2020, n.p.). In the epic war poem, *De Bello Civili* (*On the Civil War*) aka *Pharsalia*, written by Roman poet Lucan, and translated and published into English, by Thomas May in the 1620s and 30s, these lines appear, "... Whose charming voice and matchless musick mov'd/ The savage beasts, the stones, and senseless trees" (Martin, 2020, n.p.). May's career-defining work is a translated narrative of the fall of the Roman republic and the Civil Wars in the era between Pompey and Julius Caesar concerning the loss of Republican liberty, while condemning Caesar's personal ambition. May's translations first appeared in 1626, and the books used dedications as propaganda to support prominent English noblemen, who were opponents of Charles I's, and who May compared to patrician heroes of Lucan's doomed republic. The books were popular enough to have probably been read by Congreve, a classical scholar familiar with both Lucan and May. The lines are too similar to have no connection, the odds of two people independently connecting three exact things to music (breasts/beasts, rock and trees) appear insignificant, especially when May's work had been around almost seventy years and reprinted so many times (Martin, 2020). Hicks (1984) believed the problem was not beasts/breasts but "our need to define music itself," because if music is a simple process of tone-pitch, timbre or consonance, then even animals are affected by it, just as listening to the ugly sounds (music) that pass for English fox hunting songs, something definitely non-native to the woods, may scare (charm) the animal out and get the beast killed.

Beats & Brain Cells

If music is a rational ordering of sounds into melody, texture and other musical terms, which creates a perception of structure to create a whole bigger than the sum of its parts, then music arises from complicated mixtures of individual sounds. "The crux of this discussion, then, is between the rational and the irrational," (Hicks, 1984, p. 54) the question is not whether music is "powerful or charming enough to soothe the savage breast," (Hicks, 1984, p. 54) or even if beasts are rational enough to enjoy it but "whether we are rational enough to decide what, after all, music is" (Hicks, 1984, p. 54). Auditory processing starts in the cochlea of the inner ear, where sound waves are perceived by sensory hair cells and then conveyed to the CNS by spiral ganglion neurons, which reliably maintain the frequency, intensity and timing of each stimulus. "During the assembly of auditory circuits, spiral ganglion neurons establish precise connections that link hair cells in the cochlea to target neurons in the auditory brainstem, develop specific firing properties, and elaborate unusual synapses both in the periphery and in the CNS" (Appler & Goodrich, 2011, p. 488). Comprehending how spiral ganglion neurons develop these singular properties is a fundamental goal in auditory neuroscience, since these neurons are the sole input of auditory information to the brain. Appler and Goodrich (2011) wrote that until recently studies of the auditory system have trailed behind other CNS sensory systems due to the limited size and inaccessibility to the inner ear, but with new molecular genetic tools, the science is catching up.

America's oldest teenager, Dick Clark, is often credited with saying "Music is the soundtrack of your life." (Brinkworth, 2012, n.p.) In saying music has the power, the emphasis becomes that music has an ability to transform your mental state, this idea is similar to the quote by Lin Yutang, "What is patriotism but the love of the food one ate as a child?" (Yutang, 1998, p. 46). In this vein patriotism is nostalgia and often prompted by music. Michael Jackson once stated that in listening to a piece of music for the first time one should do it in a quiet room with headphones on and that if you did not like the song almost immediately then you do not *like* the song. Jackson explained that the reason most people like music is not because of the music itself, but because of the ambiance, the vibes and being entrained to like the song. Many music listeners hear the same music habitually, usually hearing it in specific locations doing specific actions, Bergland (2017) writes that "we all have personal anthems and favorite music that will forever remind us of memorable periods in our lives," (n.p.). An African coworker of mine used to sing the song "Tootsie Roll" by the 69 Boyz which was a popular song in the nightclubs he and his friends frequented, he was dismayed when asked what he was singing because he believed everyone had heard the song. Now whether the song in and of itself was a "good" song did not matter, to him the song represented good times he was having in America, this is a common occurrence where we listen to music in a certain venue that creates a particular state of mind. Bergland (2017) asks what songs do you immediately think of as your all-time favorite or the one-hit wonders that leave that unerasable earworm on your mind? People tend to equate the neurochemical response of the total gestalt with the individual parts, in this instance the music is thought of as having charm, Robert Sapolksy would say it could have been something you ate or ingested. Music programs you from infancy to death throughout your life.

Set, Setting & Sound

What would be the playlist of songs that could tell your life story, what final cut of your life soundtrack would charm the savage beast and how much would be auditory stimulation of memories stored in the CNS? Wilkins et al. (2015) write that "Most people choose to listen to music that they prefer or 'like'," (p. 1) with earlier research concentrating on how different genres of music affect the brain. While listening to their favorite music, no matter what genre, people often report re-experiencing personal thoughts and memories, and why this happens in the CNS remains hazy, emotions are caused by cascades of neurochemicals that wash across your brain and through your CNS. After ingesting several hundred micrograms of the neurochemical LSD_{25} in 1985, a synesthesia-like state was experienced that informs my current perspective to this day, even with limited research in this area much has been learned about how external neurochemicals can act as agonists, antagonists or even partial agonists like 5-HT2A, which is a serotonin 2A type receptor, or a receptor for the neurochemical serotonin. Individual people are deterministic mechanisms composed of individual atoms, molecules, cells, tissues, organs, and organ systems, with the central nervous system (CNS) being one, comprised of a spinal cord and a brain, made up of neurons, dendrites, axons and scores of receptors. Even after directly experiencing the effects of LSD_{25} it took me years to be able to put a name to many of the ideas experienced in 1985, continuing through a higher level education today. Most people live in the immediate level, experiencing the whole and not the sum of its parts, often failing to grok the macro or micro levels of reality, blinded by the light, blinded by the Game, blinded by what is actually occurring, without grasping the intricacies.

Wilkins et al. (2015) used network science methods, to evaluate differences in functional brain connectivity when individual people listened to entire songs and appeared to demonstrate that a circuit believed to be important for internally-focused thoughts, called the default mode network (DMN) or resting-state network, fired the most when listening to favorite or liked music. Most music is listened to in the moment, which links it to the situation and many scientists would like to separate universally inspirational music from momentary anthems. Wilkins et al. (2015) also seemed to find that listening to a favorite song changes the connectivity between auditory brain areas and the hippocampus, a region that appears responsible for calling up autobiographical memories, fantasizing, and stream of consciousness mind-wandering. Because musical tastes differ from individual to individual and music can range in acoustic complexity, with or without lyrics, the consistency of Wilkins et al. (2015) results was surprising and may explain why similar emotional and mental states can be felt by people listening to music as dissimilar as Beethoven and the 69 Boyz. When your soundtrack of life engages the DMN it is like reliving the past and if the songs conjure up affirmative memories it releases neurochemicals to make you feel satisfied, in other words, sound waves strike the tympanic membranes, which send neurochemical signals to your CNS and produce certain effects, typically referred to as emotions.

All I Wanted Was a Pepsi

In the film Ratatouille (2007) the character Anton Ego states that being critical is easy because very little is risked in tearing others apart and the work they put forth, just as some criminologists live to produce negative criticism. In the field of criminology small pleasures exist in pointing out the absurdities in mainstream criminology, especially the look on the faces of those that so blindly believe in the archeology/genealogy of Western white supremacist, Beccarian criminology. This defense of determinism is founded on fMRI studies done over the last decade, my personal experiences with criminology and the soundtrack of life and this is where the risk of the "new" comes into play because as Ego states, "The world is often unkind to new talent, new creations. The new needs friends" (Marcbranches, 2009). As an Atheist, Anarchist criminologist my perspective is grounded in a scientific method, which to clarify does not mean that because an individual or group calls their research scientific, it makes it so; criticism and skepticism remain foundational in radical criminology. My radical critical perspective does not create nor preserve the current mainstream criminology, that is not my imperative or prerogative, the best analogy is the Hindu pantheon of Brahma the Creator or Vishnu the Preserver. From the beginning of my formal criminological education professors and colleagues have stressed the need for presenting both sides of the argument, but my criminological perspective hones closer to Shiva the Destroyer, aka the Lord of Creation, who's very act of destruction allows for creation, with little to no need to present both sides.

My criminological perspective is not one which explains how to build a better prison or to make the legal system more palatable, but to assail the criminology that keeps the modern prison-industrial complex in play, beginning with its most fundamental building block, the individual human. From a radical critical perspective, it must be understood that there is always a Game, something going on and something being pushed, a perspective, a narrative, a point of view. Take musical education in schools, some of the main pieces learned are patriotic pieces such as "The Star-Spangled Banner" because the band plays it before the beginning of every football game as the flag is raised on the pole. This radical critical influence was developed by growing up in West Texas at the end of the Juan Crow era which was not understandable to my developing mind at that time, but upon joining the US Army and seeing racism, bigotry and collaboration so blatantly displayed, not only from whites, but from blacks and Puerto Ricans as well. Growing up in West Texas in the 1960s and 1970s also had advantages of formal education funded by petroleum taxes at a time when school bands were just waning in popularity, but due to the size of the school almost all students participated in learning to play an instrument in both marching and orchestral settings. My education was the equivalent of an upper middle-class education with school-sponsored field trips hundreds of miles away to the Carlsbad Caverns, UIL events and Shakespearean plays at the Globe of the Great Southwest, a simplified and modernized version of the larger Elizabethan Globe. These programs were descendants of the New Deal and the National Endowment for the Arts, powered by pre-Robin Hood West Texas Intermediate Crude dollars, with the ideology that learning arts made a better society. A formal education teaches a student the propaganda necessary to obey, which is understood, even if decried by traditional conservatives and dog whistle blowers when this is pointed out to them, or worse they dig in and defend it as necessary to patriotism. American educators truly believe in the dictum, "Give me a child till he is seven years old, and I will show you the man," said, Ignatius Loyola (CommonWeal, 2016). This education is now vilified as the teachings of dead white male supremacists yet learning how to play music now gives me a better understanding and appreciation of all forms of music across the world allowing me to develop an eclectic taste, some of which includes hip-hop.

The Soundtrack of Your Life

One must learn to play the notes, chords and structures, yet the language of music is not defined by the Western world, but by a rational mind as Hicks (1984) wrote. The mythology of someone like Miles Davis is that he learned music from a very young age and then went to what is now the Juilliard School of Music where he learned European notated, classical music, while at night in the Big Apple, the 18-year old Davis played the more improvisational African-American jazz. He eventually dropped out of Julliard but always claimed afterwards that the classical fundamentals he learned at Julliard helped him understand music better and made him a better musician, many of the greatest musicians in the world learned scales and chords in the beginning. The mythology persists that Miles Davis followed Charlie "Bird" Parker around wanting to learn from him, but not many know the story of how Charlie Parker supposedly followed Edgard Varèse so that he could teach the great Bird more. Varèse was an influence on a 15-year old Frank Zappa, who found Varèse's phone number by calling Information on the phone and asking for Edgard Varèse in Greenwich Village. Varèse was also a classically trained musician who in the early 1900s believed new instruments were needed "very badly" and even without the "new instruments," Varèse spent years crafting proto-electronic music for live musicians, using percussion and conventional instruments to create great sound masses, non-Western harmonies and noise-based music which today sounds like it could have been made using a Roland TR-808 or DX7 and an orchestra. What each of the preceding musicians has, is a formal education in music, and this seems important if one is to learn as a subject well.

The genealogy of hip-hop is still being decided so the archaeology continues, but proto-hip-hop existed as far back as the 1960s in New York City and as of this writing the movement traces its origins to The Bronx. Afrika Bambaataa laid out the main pillars of hip hop culture as: (1) orality—rapping/

MCing/emceeing" by using a rhythmic vocal rhyming style, (2) sound/musicality—DJing/turntablism, making music with record players/electronic equipment, (3) movement/dance -b-boying/b-girling/breakdancing and (4) art—through the use of graffiti. Beyond the main four are: intellectual/philosophical knowledge of hip hop culture and the movement, knowing the percussive vocal style of beatboxing, street hustling, hip hop language, hip hop fashion and style, among others. Hip hop has a contentious genealogy with Blanchard (1999) writing "Hip-hop music originated from a combination of traditionally African-American forms of music...created by working-class African-Americans...to invent a new form of music that both expressed and shaped the culture of black New York City youth in the 1970s," (n.p.). A decade later Forman (2010) would write, "Despite its contemporary expansion and appeal across racial and cultural sectors, hip-hop is an unambiguously African-American cultural phenomenon that emerges within a complex amalgam of hybrid social influences," (n.p.). This history, like much of history in America, is a shaped narrative, a retelling or what is commonly referred to as a white lie. Blanchard (1999) wrote that while much of the original innovations that came to be known as hip-hop music began in New York working class neighborhoods it was soon co-opted and commodified by white business interests by forcing African-American AM stations that had begun the hip-hop music culture in the 1970s, out of the market. With the corporatization of hip-hop culture by mainly white interests came the focus on commercializing the music and the erasure of the other pillars of hip-hop, which were a product of Latino culture (Skluzak & Tate, 2004). Skluzak and Tate (2004) write that while Latinos in the beginning were overwhelmingly Puerto Rican the difficulty of racial categorization helped with their erasure out of hip-hop history and since in the beginning MCing and DJing were what became the music industry and had been dominated by African-Americans, the other pillars were ignored. Like the erasure of Latino history out of hip-hop, which Skluzak and Tate (2004) attribute to more than one factor, none of which are well intentioned, it remains similar to most American white supremacist revisionist history taught in most schools in America. Skluzak and Tate (2004) write that the Latino-Caribbean-African-American New York culture and neighborhoods that had created the hip-hop culture as partners were split apart by commercialization and corporate interests, a tactic perfected in the Americas since Bacon's Rebellion. This shaping of the narrative in history is why critical race theory remains crucial, and while most students know of Jim Crow Laws, fewer know of similar Anti-Chinese or Juan Crow laws. Skluzak and Tate (2004) explain that the popular conception of hip-hop is claimed as African (Thomas, 2007), and much like various tribes created from Spanish colonization, annexation and immigration, New York Puerto Ricans, key participants, producers and consumers of hip-hop culture and art forms since hip-hop's inception in the early 1970s in the South Bronx, have become excluded based on racialized pan-ethnicity. Long before anti-police hip-hop became popularized in the late 1980s/early 1990s, Mexican corrido's influenced my journey into Anarchy, even my Atheism was shaped by the Satanic Panic of the late 1970s and 1980s and English-language rock. This erasure by both the white and African-American communities is often used as a tool of divide and conquer and has happened to even my tribe in the Mexican diaspora. In a class taken for my Doctoral studies, taken at an HBCU, the professor was speaking about the erasure of the contributions made by Buffalo Soldiers in the Western US, to which I reminded them that as an individual of Indigenous/Mexican heritage my people were the ones being erased by what they believed to be heroes.

My exposure to hip-hop music happened as early as 1980 with the album "Rappers Delight" by The Sugarhill Gang through an individual of Mexican descent who would go on to become my cousin by marriage. His babysitter as a child had been an African-American woman who had taken care of him and his siblings because his father owned a produce company, and his mother was a local celebrity who hosted a Spanish-language music program on a local NBC affiliate. The caretaker had introduced him to African-American music and when we got together and rode around in his vehicle, he played different genres of African-American music. He also liked to hang out and watch "Soul Train" on Saturdays to see the new acts and we did that before heading out into the town, since they lived in the Odessa/Midland area of Texas, an hour away from the Boondocks in which I resided. My second encounter with hip hop music was in 1984 a cousin of mine, who was adopted from a white family, also from the Odessa/Midland area, acquired a mixtape of what would later become "Escape" by Whodini. He played the mixtape on auto-reverse the entire night and refused to play anything else with the excuse that it was his car, and he could play what he wanted, by the end of the night songs like "Friends" and "Five Minutes of Funk" were etched into my brain. In my small Boondocks town, I had a social circle that included African-American friends that we had grown up with and continued to party with. A couple of weeks after listening to the mixtape my friends brother Rabbit arrived at the house really excited about a new cassette that had just dropped and he went to put it on for his brother, and within a few bars I recognized "Five Minutes of Funk" and I said that it was not new it had been out. He started trash talking me telling me "Meskins" did not know anything about this kind of music and that he had just bought it brand-new from the record store. So, I began rapping along with the lyrics of the song and this really angered him, I then started singing the lyrics to "Friends" without even listening to the song, so Rabbit fast-forwarded and when he heard the song and my lyrics, he became even angrier and stormed out, as his brother who was laughing hard told Rabbit to go get his money back. According to Rabbit the music should have been exclusive to the African-American culture and a few years later while I was a slave in the Texas Gulag most African-American prisoners took this to a violent extreme. It took a while after leaving the Texas Gulag Archipelago before I began listening to hip-hop again, without it being racialized, interestingly in the Gulag I ran into Rabbit who was also doing time. One day while we were conversing as I worked in the chow line, another African-American prisoner interrupted and said something racial towards me and Rabbit turned towards him angrily and said we were friends from the outside and that if he didn't want any problems, he needed to keep his mouth shut, especially when he didn't know who he was talking about. We had become tribal after all those years of hanging and partying in the small West Texas Boondocks town.

Conclusion

My arrival in the criminology discipline has been because of my contact with the legal system and while many individuals working for PhDs have actually worked for the state's slave system in some capacity or another, I was made a slave. The field of criminology has a shaped narrative created by the slave-makers and their apologists, which is used to justify the continuing slavery of mostly the poor, uneducated or ignorant. The criminology curriculum is taught from the point of view of the slaver and proponents of slavery because the end result of modern criminology is slavery and retribution. Criminology as the discipline exists today views retribution as the norm, continuing the legacy of white supremacist treatment of people not belonging to the inner circles of American social hierarchies. It has been my personal experience that most criminologists advocate retribution which the majority equate to justice, if justice were an actual goal and concept in criminology, they would not have to create a subfield called restorative justice. Much of the ideology in current criminology arises from the mythological middle class (proletariats with aspirations) and which are under the spell of the influencer class as to how the poor's behave and should be treated. Even subgroups in criminological associations such as convict criminologists are oversaturated with individuals who are not representative of the prison-industrial complex in America and are more collaborators than allies to radical and critical criminologists.

Prison abolitionists, many of whom have never even been to prison, appear to do better work in criminology than people of color, who are often conservative collaborators. Diverse voices are beginning to ascend in criminology, but minorities are often used as color-washing for traditional, conservative ideology. Hip-hop criminology is able to bring in anti-establishment experiences which pushback against the white supremacist ideology which passes for criminology today, especially when the people of color are not traditional conservative collaborators. While critical and radical criminologists are ascending, much like a catalyst in a chemical reaction, they are a statistical anomaly that remains significant. This spoken word rap from a skate thrash band named Suicidal Tendencies will be used in conclusion, "How can you say what my best interest is? What are you trying to say, I'm crazy? When I went to your schools, I went to your churches, I went to your institutional learning facilities?! So how can you say I'm crazy?" (Blank TV, 2008).

References

Appler, J. M., & Goodrich, L. V. (2011). "Connecting the ear to the brain: Molecular mechanisms of auditory circuit assembly." *Progress in Neurobiology*, *93*(4), 488–508. Retrieved from https://www.sciencedirect.com/science/article/pii/S0301008211000050?via%3Dihub

Bergland, C. (2017). "The neuroscience of hearing the soundtracks of your life." *Psychology Today*. Retrieved from https://www.psychologytoday.com/us/blog/the-athletes-way/201704/the-neuroscience-hearing-the-soundtracks-your-life

Blanchard, B. (1999). "The social significance of rap & hip-hop culture." *Poverty & Prejudice: Media and Race*. Ethics of Development in a Global Environment (EDGE). Retrieved from http://web.stanford.edu/class/e297c/poverty_prejudice/mediarace/socialsignificance.htm

Blank TV. (2008, Feb 23). *Suicidal Tendencies—"Institutionalized" Frontier Records – Official Music Video*. [Video]. YouTube. Retrieved from https://www.youtube.com/watch?v=LoF_a0-7xVQ&ab_channel=BlankTV

Brinkworth, D. (2012). "Music is the soundtrack of your life" Airman & Family Readiness Center. Ellsworth Air Force Base, South Dakota. Retrieved from https://ellsworthafrc.org/2012/04/20/music-is-the-soundtrack-of-your-life/

CommonWeal. (2016). "Give me a child till he is seven years old." *Source*. Retrieved from https://sourcenews.scot/give-me-a-child-till-he-is-seven-years-old/

Fitch, W. T. (2005). "The evolution of music in comparative perspective." *Annals of the New York Academies of Sciences*, *1060*, 29–49. Retrieved from doi:10.1196/annals.1360.004

Forman, M. (2010). "Conscious hip-hop, change, and the Obama era." *American Studies Journal.* No. 54. Retrieved from http://www.asjournal.org/54-2010/conscious-hip-hop/

Hicks, M. (1984). "Soothing the savage beast: A note on animals and music." *The Journal of Aesthetic Education, 18*(4), 47–55. Retrieved from https://tsuhhelweb.tsu.edu:2075/stable/pdf/3332626.pdf?ab_segments=0%252Fbasic_search%252Fcontrol&refreqid=excelsior%3A2a5f76061cb990d07d83dd6b690eb51d

Marcbranches. (2009, Mar 19). *Ratatouille – Anton Ego speech.* [Video]. YouTube. Retrieved from https://www.youtube.com/watch?v=-JPOoFkrh94&ab_channel=-marcbranches

Martin, G. (2020). "Music has charms to soothe the savage breast." *The Phrase Finder.* Retrieved from https://www.phrases.org.uk/meanings/music-has-charms-to-soothe-the-the-savage-breast.html

Merker, B. (2000)." Synchronous chorusing and human origins." In N. L. Wallin, B. Merker, & S. Brown (Eds.), *The origins of music* (pp. 315–327). Cambridge, MA: The MIT Press.

Skluzak, D., & Tate, T. (2004). *Latino hip-hop!* Retrieved from http://websites.umich.edu/~ac213/student_projects06/student_projects/lhh/images/overview.html

Thomas, A. (2007). "The spirit and philosophy of Hip Hop." *The New Statesman.* Retrieved from https://www.newstatesman.com/culture/music-theatre/2007/09/hip-hop-movements-thought

Wilkins, R., Hodges, D., Laurienti, P., Steen, M., & Burdette, J. H. (2015). Network science and the effects of music preference on functional brain connectivity: From Beethoven to Eminem. *Science Reports* 4. Art. No. Retrieved from https://doi.org/10.1038/srep06130

Yutang, L. (1998). *The importance of living.* New York, NY: William Morris Paperbacks.

Stop and Search: Representations of Police Harassment in British Hip Hop during the 1980s

ADAM DE PAOR-EVANS

Introduction

During recent times in Britain, it has been extensively reported in the media that members of Black communities have experienced high levels of police harassment. Under the UK Government's stop and search policy—a policy first rising to national prominence during the Brixton riots in 1981—Black people are 9.5 times more likely to be stopped than white people (Gov.uk, 2020). Furthermore, the overall stop and search figures have almost doubled since to turn of the millennium. A growing sense of activism aiming to combat the ingrained structural racism in Britain—perpetuated by the international Black Lives Matter (BLM) movement and the national Windrush scandal—has also grown out of the disturbing data and harrowing experiences of many Black people's experience of stop and search, a policy which has recurringly been accused of constituting police harassment and police brutality.

One of the most explicit metaphors of the recent counterattack on systemic racism is represented through the events of the BLM protest in Bristol on 7th June 2020, when a statue of Edward Colston was toppled from its Portland stone plinth, splattered with red paint, rolled along the street, and hurled into the water at Bristol Harbour. Colston, a Member of Parliament in the Conservative Party, made a fortune due to his involvement in the Atlantic slave trade, and by the late seventeenth century was deputy governor of the Royal African Company, an English mercantile trading company who were responsible for shipping more African slaves to the Americas than any other in the Atlantic slave trade's history. This metaphoric dismantling of racist hierarchies is hugely significant, both locally and nationally. Locally, the city of Bristol is home to a rich mix of music culture and heritage, not least due to its deep reggae presence, built from the sound system culture born in the 1960s, growing out of the calypso and mento sounds that Caribbean immigrants brought to the city a decade before. Reggae sound systems continued to take a central role when the formative sounds of hip hop arrived from New York, and The Wild Bunch—the Bristol-based crew which morphed in Massive Attack—practiced hip hop with the ethos of sound system culture. Bristol has always been a place of creative resistance against institutional prejudices. The African Caribbean community protested against the Bristol Omnibus Company racist employment policy in 1963 and following two months of dispute the actions of the community contributed to establishing the Race Relations Act 1968. Similarly, with the Colston protest, the actions of the demonstrators have led to a wider shift in thinking about certain components of systemic racism, some of which are embedded in forms of representation. Since Colston was rolled into the water, major music venue Colston Hall has been renamed Bristol Beacon, and Colston's Girls' School renamed Montpelier High School.

However, it is not just the recent events of the BLM movement that have fueled an opening up of the racism conversation. Whilst BLM has been explicit in bringing the ingrained existence of racism to the fore, for decades protestors have attempted to open up conversation about empire, racism, and slavery and its associated day-to-day societal issues of police harassment and brutality, and some of the clearest representations of protest lie in hip hop songs. The aim of this chapter is to critically present the evidence of police brutality and harassment—often cloaked behind the stop and search policy—through extensive lyric, theoretical, and contextual analysis of hip hop songs in Britain, focusing on the individual encounter. The chapter concludes by attesting that although a highly visible current issue, the past negative experiences of Black communities in Britain are also palpable, and that these rap songs bring visibility to victims of structural racism. Finally, the chapter positions the formative work of British hip hop artists from the margins to a take a more central space in the socio-politics of hip hop history.

The Arrival of Hip Hop and 1980s Britain

Hip hop landed in Britain during the early 1980s, propelled on its transatlantic journey by Malcolm McLaren and The World's Famous Supreme Team's "Buffalo Gals" (1982) extravaganza, the year following the Brixton riots. Whilst this new, exciting youth culture exploded across Britain and captured the imaginations and energy of a generation, what was at its core was still an emerging part of the processes of hip hop. Although breakdancing had become an overnight sensation, its inherent practice that preserves the intangible cultures of traditional African dance forms was as much unknown in Britain as it was a contemporaneous creative discipline for addressing gang warfare in New York City.

Whilst the youth were grappling with the four tangible elements of hip hop—its fifth element still out of reach for many—the new political philosophy of Thatcherism had firmly taken root as Thatcher won a landslide victory in the summer of 1983. Whilst the newly-formed SDP–Liberal Alliance were blamed for splitting opposition support with the Labour Party and thus enabling Thatcher to easily achieve a majority, however, additionally significant contributing factors were the Conservatives policies on employment, economic growth, and defense. The defense rhetoric was propelled by Britain's victory in the Falklands War, which saw a rise in British sovereignty among the population, which, in part, fueled a nationalist mindset. Colonialist thinking turned inwards and a rise in racism became apparent with the formation of John Tyndall's British National Party (BNP), which sought to fight its cause through street marches and rallies (Combat 18 paramilitary—its name a coded reference to Nazi German leader Adolf Hitler—to protect its events from anti-fascist protesters) rather than on a political stage. Whilst the BNP took to the streets—the biggest spatial trope in hip hop—they were also the places of tentative yet emerging hip hop practice, as school playgrounds, shopping precincts, and unused public space saw youths breakdancing by day, while the graffiti phenomenon gradually soaked the country by night. The streets were also the space where the practices of stop and search were carried out, a space where even now the relationship between levels of stop and search and reductions of crime seems insubstantial (Quinton et al., 2017).

British hip hop adopters' understanding of the idea of knowledge as the fifth element of hip hop was introduced through the Afrofuturist-driven soundscapes of Afrika Bambaataa and Soulsonic Force's "Looking for The Perfect Beat" and "Renegades of Funk", the latter explicit in its celebration of Black revolutionaries who challenged the racist structures of socio-politics. As docufiction films such as *Wild Style, Style Wars, Beat Street,* and the more commercially appealing *Breakdance: The Movie* (renamed from *Breakin'* for the UK audience) were pivotal in bringing the British youth insights into the world of hip hop praxes, it was Dick Fontaine's 1984 documentary *Beat This! A Hip Hop History* that affirmed the strength of knowledge as the core essence of hip hop culture, and the concept of knowing one's past to determine one's future. However, the consciousness associated with being a rapper was already in existence in Britain, with London-based funk band Funkapolitan introducing rap into their music in 1981 (and launching London's first rap club the Language Lab). Additionally, Newtrament's "London Bridge is Falling Down" (1983) was the first British hip hop record to address socio-political issues and the constant threat of nuclear war.

Police Brutality on Wax

Whilst Public Enemy were arguably the first crew to bring an explicit awareness of systemic racism to broader audiences through their seminal debut album *Yo! Bum Rush The Show* (1987), it was N.W.A. who overtly attacked police brutality through songs like "___ The Police (Fill In The Blanks)" (1988). However, tensions between Black communities and the police have been represented in hip hop songs since the dawn of the 1980s, most prominently by the scene at the close of "The Message" (1982), which sees the crew accosted by police patrol. In the music video, we see five members of the crew hanging out, sympathizing with "Betty", whose "moms got robbed man…She got hurt bad", when a patrol car swerves to the curb and two police officers aggressively rush from the car to the crew—hands on pistols and waving truncheons—as one officer yells "Freeze! Don't nobody move nothin', y'all know what this is", and the other "Get 'em up, get 'em up!". A protesting voice explains: "Yo man, we're down with Grandmaster Flash and The Furious Five, man", to which one officer retorts "Who's that, a gang?". The two other crew members appear—asking "Officer, what's the problem?" which receives the reply "You the problem!". All seven crew members are bundled in the patrol vehicle, as the closing shot zooms into the flashing lights atop the police car while sirens and the music fade. Whilst this sequence acts as a kind of epilogue to the core narrative, its representation of police harassment is significant. Into the 1990s, rap songs that took issue with police misconduct not only documented and attested to the breadth of this appalling practice, but they also widened awareness of these deeply ingrained societal problems to a more expansive audience.

Three exemplary records that address structural racism and police brutality in terms of strategy, community, and the individual, are Main Source's "Just a Friendly Game of Baseball" (1991), Brand Nubian's "Claimin' I'm a Criminal" (1994), and "The Headcracker" (1992) by Double XX Posse. In "Just a Friendly Game of Baseball", Large Professor illustrates police brutality at the strategic level of the police force as his lyrics exhaust the baseball metaphor. Police ploys are compared to baseball tactics, as "The bases are loaded", because "to the cops, shootin' brothers is like playin' baseball"; he also compares body count motifs "I guess when they shoot up a crew, it's a grand slam / And when it's one, it's a home run". Large Pro clearly infers the systemically racist socio-political structures, where "The umpires are the government", who will remove by design any police officer who challenges the strategy: "I guess they took him out the game, and replace him / With a pinch-hitter, in the scam he was a quitter". Furthermore, "Just a Friendly Game of Baseball" also points to the embedded double-standards and discrimination within baseball culture (Christiano, 1986; Lipsitz, 2006), by subverting the Black Sox tag, thus reinforcing the nature of systemic racism. Brand Nubian's "Claimin' I'm a Criminal" tackles police brutality as it targets Black neighbourhoods. Taking its title and a subtle vocal sample of a Chuck D lyric from "Don't Believe the Hype" (1988), the song recounts a narrative of an early morning police raid, suggesting that this could happen to any member of the Black community as: "It's the whole Black race that they're fuckin' with". Double XX Posse's "The Headcracker" addresses the individual's experience of police brutality, from the spoken work intro: "Yo man, lemme tell you what happened to me the other night, right? I was at my man's house watching the basketball game...Stepped outside to the store, the police rolled up on me and told me I wilded somebody!" The rap ensues, recounting a story where: "Then out of nowhere the cops rolled up and said / 'Put your hands up' I said, 'What the fuck?' / The Headcracker"; stating "This is a bad situation just because I'm Black". The story relates back to the essence of systemic racism in the closing lines, illustrating the harrowingly real impact of ingrained structural prejudice.

The British Voice

The previous section presented a small sample of US hip hop records that clearly attest to the Black lives in America that experienced the recurring problem of police brutality and harassment in the 1980s and 1990s, but what of Britain? What follows is an analysis of British hip hop and dancehall records that express comparable experiences to their US contemporaries, but from a Black British perspective that situates systemic racism within the frame of formative British hip hop culture and British socio-politics. Since the mid-1980s, London-centric British hip hop has thrived on a close intertwining with the sound and culture of British sound systems and dancehall deejays, which was crucial to forming the identity of British hip hop of the time as a separate entity to that of the US. The influence of Jamaican and Caribbean culture is apparent throughout the songs discussed that follow, which includes work from Sir Drew & Rapski, Demon Boyz, London Posse,

Silent Eclipse, Son of Noise, and dancehall legends Peter King and Smiley Culture.

Sir Drew & Rapski's "Notting Hill" (1987) delivers a clear account of police harassment. Once the beat drops, a narrative similar to the cessation in "The Message" ensues, with two police officers accosting the crew, first inquiring "I've got a belief you got illegal substance on your person?" and the second demanding spitefully: "Empty yer pockets!" before the sluggish chanted hook "Notting Hill / We're talking about the bill". The first verse opens with an introduction to Ladbroke Grove and Notting Hill, an area of West London with a history of race riots and slum landlords exploiting Caribbean immigrant tenants. Following this brief framing, Rapski expresses: "Well I've been living in The Grove for such a long time / And I can't even go on the front line / 'Cause if I do I see the Babylon / They'll grab me by the hand and put me in the van / And once in the van they'll hit me with a truncheon". The sparseness of the rap, devoid of much material description, contains a blunt honesty which presents the reality of the everyday; an everyday loaded with racial tension often resulting in being stopped and searched. The "Notting Hill / we're talking about the bill", hook repeats four times after each verse, bridging an apparent switch-up from the individual experiences of systemic racism to pure hip hop rap tropes: "I'm Rapski and I'm here to stay / At the top and there's no way that you're ever gonna stop me / If I try to go for my ambition / Don't try to stop me 'cause I'm a musician / And I've got to, got to, make you rock on / All night long until the break of dawn".

However, the juxtaposition of these lyrics with the stop and search story presented in the first verse coupled with the hook suggests a closer relationship with the subject matter of police harassment. Rapski's proclamation that he is "here to stay" illustrates a sureness in his presence, not only within the British hip hop scene but within British society as a whole; Rapski confronts the police as much as his hip hop rivals, in that "there's no way that you're ever gonna stop me" stakes his sociocultural counter position to the heinous practices of structural racism. By flowing back into the hip hop tropes proper, Rapski's rockin' on "All night long until the break of dawn" is, at face value, an inadvertent flip back into token rap phraseology, but is an insightful sleight of hand dismissal of the police, attesting his resilience to such structural tactics. In *Provincial Headz* (2020: 253–254), I discussed "Hip Hop/Reggae Connection'", Rapski's building on his use of the term "Babylon" and further contextualizing London's Jamaican influence on "Hip Hop/Reggae Connection" (1987) which fuses Caribbean "terminologies with common hip hop tropes", a stylistic approach to lyric writing and delivery archetypal of

Stop and Search: Representations of Police Harassment

London artists Demon Boyz, Asher D & Daddy Freddy, and London Posse, all of whom have expressed narratives connected to police harassment.

Demon Boyz "Law Abiding Citizen" (1992) delivers a narrative over a half-bar chop of Funk Inc.'s "Kool is Back" (1971) and Fred Wesley and the J.B.s' "More Peas" (1973) bassline, that firstly reflects on the Tottenham riots in 1985, the mistrust between the Black community and the police force, and stop and search. Mike J and Demon D each launch their own takes on police harassment: Mike J opens with "I used to be a law abiding citizen", where he would regularly go about his business "Daily / Nuff of the police dem in a Tottenham dem try to provoke me", before declaring the police "only uphold the law when it means raiding, arresting, spot-checking", and continues to argue that the police are not prepared to support the Black community where there are problems, but rather, "On the Black youth the police are putting on too much tension". He concludes by depicting the social imbalance in terms of cocaine and crack dealers "Running pon the street who are kill their friends / Why don't you leave the Blacks bwoy, and look fi dem?". Demon D recounts an experience walking from a bar with friends in the street, when he is approached by the Criminal Investigation Department: "It's the CID man check it like Rambo", who throw him onto the car bonnet then: "Open up mi jacket then them pull all mi zips", and continue to search him based on nothing more than stereotypical profiling: "So you a search me and interrogate me / Invade my property steal my integrity". He counters the officers by quoting the presumption of innocence (Stumer, 2010), concluding his verse with: "A man is innocent until proven guilty / So when I'm on the streets I expect to be free".

In "Live Like the Other Half Do" (1989), Bionic describes himself as a "daily roughneck", and also the "prime suspect", and a victim of circumstance stating: "When I'm in the vicinity of a robbery" he receives harassment purely as he is Black. Although innocent, the police's nonchalant and racist approach prompts an arrest, as: "one nigga looks as good as any other", promoting a disregard for both identity and mistaken identity. Bionic attests the impact of such negative experiences and impact on mental health "Another day of racist police brutality / And this reality has changed my personality". MCD focuses on the broken system on the epic "The Damned" (1993), before bringing the question "Mr. Officer, I wanna know, why you wanna nick me when I'm on the go? / Excuse me Mr. Officer I don't know why / You don't like Black guys you don't seem wise". Repeated through the 16-bar stanza, the "Mr. Officer" hook repeats eight times, the fifth relating back to the problems of a corrupt system, suggesting "Mr. Officer you got the wrong guy no doubt / The guy you're looking for is in a white house". Whilst the obvious points to The White House and redolent of transatlantic corruption, or The White House as metaphor of top-down systematic failure, MCD's use carries a double-meaning whereby the emphasis is the reality of a white house as a place for cocaine dealing. Hence, the argument is that the police would rather stop and search members of the Black community than raid a cocaine den, the dealers of which are often the subject of agent-centred corruption, particularly "when the relationship between officer and informant is effectively reversed" (Moran, 2005: 61). A similar scenario is presented in "Here the Cop" (1995) by Son of Noise, within which Curoc reflects on his school days in 1987, and frames a context laden with racial tensions, where race wars led to racist whites being forgiven yet "Blacks were locked up", "Criminal minded, blinded by the system / Caught up in a world of hate, another victim". The relationship between the institutional structural racism and the impact on the personal-individual is clear.

Returning to the Jamaican influence, Peter King's "Step on the Gas (Hit the Road Don)" (1985) presents a story where the central idea sees Peter pursued by a police vehicle whilst driving his brother's loaned shabby car. With a comedic hint, the plot unfolds through a series of recurring motifs where Peter must pull over and ask one of his passengers to get out of the vehicle to enable him to drive faster and away from the police. Eventually, Peter turns into a dead end street, and acting fast leaps out before the vehicle trundles into a brick wall. Whilst regarding the wreck, the police—unknowing that Peter has bailed out the car—"Like a rocket, followed it / Smashed the windscreen, and did the bonnet". Whilst the listener can imagine this scenario in an almost slapstick manner—largely due to Peter's lyric composition and delivery—the sinister undertone carried throughout the song strikes a harrowing chord at its conclusion. The listener is left conjecturing the outcome had Peter not leapt from the vehicle, and its disturbing potential consequences.

A similar scenario is played out by Smiley Culture (fellow deejay of Peter King in Saxon Sound System) in his 1984 autobiographical song "Police Officer". Smiley received commercial success with three singles reaching the UK Official Singles Chart, and his lyrical content contextualized a range of linguistic and materialistic tropes of identity in multicultural Britain and the Commonwealth (Robinson, 2021). Also delivering a core idea centred on being pulled over while driving, "Police Officer" retells Smiley's story through a comedic approach, but from the first line Smiley announces that "Every time me drive me car police a stop me superstar"—which calls into question why—particularly as he continues to inform the listener that "True me drive a Fiat and a Mercs, sell weh me Lancia", suggesting the reason for accosting is the driver and not an issue with the vehicle. Smiley presents his counter position to threats of stop and search, by relating situations where police would "get run over", or he would "just drive faster", and it would be on Smiley's terms if he chose to stop and address the situation: "And when me feel like it me would a pull up on a corner / Before you ask any question me already have an answer". These first verses frame the context for the plot whereby en route to People's Club, Smiley is flagged down by "six or seven plain clothes police officers", who ensue to fire questions about his whereabouts, destination, and possessions on his person. Condescendingly addressing him as "son", "lad", and then following Smiley's offer for them to search the boot, the retort: "Shut your bloody mouth, we ask, you answer", the situation becomes more aggressive, and from Smiley's position: "But me try handle them coarse, them just handle me coarser". It transpires the police are seeking ganja and cornered under the threat of arrest and further abuse, Smiley presents his cannabis. In a final attempt to avoid arrest, Smiley announces "you can't do that ca' me name Smiley Culture", to which one officer becomes starstruck at the idea of meeting the artist famed for the 1984 hit record "Cockney Translation" (rereleased in 1985 following the success of "Police Officer"), a song with an appeal outside the dancehall fraternity, largely due to its "contrasting the Jamaican of the immigrants with the local Cockney" (Kerswill, 2014). The conclusion to the plot is that Smiley is freed in exchange for his autograph, as in reference to "Cockney Translation" the awestricken officer exclaims: "My kids love it and so does my mother!".

Although both Peter King and Smiley Culture's songs discussed above are framed in a humorous manner, the message remains as serious, a seriousness amplified by the death of Smiley Culture on 15th March 2011, during a police raid at his home in Warlingham, Surrey. An inquest jury returned a majority verdict that: "David Victor Emmanuel [Smiley's birth name] took his own life." (BBC News, 2013). A Scotland Yard spokesperson released a statement, saying: "The inquest heard how a seemingly calm situation unexpectedly escalated into an incident which was to have the most tragic of consequences" (BBC News, 2013), and in an interview with Channel 4, Merlin Emmanuel (known to the UK hip hop community as Merlin, an early British emcee), declared that the police had "failed miserably" (Channel 4, 2011). Merlin continued: "What I do know beyond reasonable doubt is that Smiley would still be alive had they not gone and executed that warrant at his house." The Independent Police Complaints Commission recommended no disciplinary action yet released this statement: "Four experienced officers felt it appropriate to detain a suspect in the kitchen, potentially the most dangerous room in the house, and afforded him a level of freedom not normally associated with an operation of this kind." The IPCC also added: "The IPCC has made a series of recommendations to the Metropolitan Police following this investigation, presenting them with areas that should be reviewed and changed in light of the findings" (BBC News, 2013). Coroner Richard Travers stated that he would suggest: "changes to the way police supervised prisoners during searches." (BBC News, 2013). At the time of writing, the situation surrounding Smiley Culture's death remains unadvanced.

Conclusion

Through its extensive lyric and contextual analysis of hip hop and dancehall records, this chapter has explored the historic personal narratives that present both individual accounts and broader Black communities experiences of the stop and search policy in Britain. These accounts, delivered through the medium of lyrics, record these events as a counter position to the rhetoric of the government agencies who support the stop and search policy. Moreover, these songs document the intangible and ephemeral personal and collective feelings towards a policy which arguably epitomizes the ingrained systemic racism that exists in the structures of British government and society. The analysis of this collection of seven songs serves as a much needed reminder of the problems with the stop and search policy inherent since its inception in 1981, as much as it is a documentation of these artists' personal histories and observations. Furthermore, although these songs were written between 29 and 40 years ago, sadly their stories and messages still resonate deeply not only through a reflective lens, but across the contemporary sociopolitical landscape of Britain.

References

Dresser, Madge. (1986). *Black and White on the buses* (pp. 47–50). Bristol: Bristol Broadsides. ISBN 0-906944-30-9.

Christiano, K. J. (1986). Salary discrimination in Major League Baseball: The effect of race. *Sociology of Sport Journal, 3*(2), 144–153.

Lipsitz, G. (2006). *The possessive investment in whiteness: How white people profit from identity politics*. Temple University Press.

Kerswill, P. (2014). The objectification of "Jafaican": the discoursal embedding of Multicultural London English in the British media. *Mediatization and sociolinguistic change*, 428–455.

Robinson, L. (2021). Smiley culture: A hybrid voice for the Commonwealth. In *Narratives from beyond the UK Reggae Bassline* (pp. 101–123). Cham: Palgrave Macmillan.

Chase, J., Fletcher, E., Glover, M., & Robinson, S. (1982). The message [Recorded by Grand Master Flash & The Furious Five Feat.: Melle Mel & Duke Bootee]. [Vinyl]. New York, NY: Sugar Hill Records.

Demon Boyz. (1992). Law abiding citizen [Recorded by Demon Boyz]. On original guidance: The Second Chapter [vinyl]. London: Tribal Bass Records.

MCD. (1993). The damned [Recorded by The Principle Feat. Silent Eclipse]. [Vinyl]. London, England: Blueprint Records.

Nicholas, A., Norbert, E., Plange, K., & Woodburn, J. (1987). Notting Hill [Recorded by Sir Drew & Rapski] On Known 2 be Down [vinyl]. London, England: Positive Beat Records.

Double XX Posse. (1992). The Headcracker [Recorded by Double XX Posse]. [Vinyl]. New York, NY: Big Beat.

DeChalus, L., & Murphy, D. (1994). Claimin' I'm a criminal [Recorded by Brand Nubian]. On everything is everything [vinyl]. New York, NY: Elektra.

Son of Noise. (1995). Here the Cop [Recorded by Son of Noise]. On Access Denied. Bullsh*t & Politics Pt. 1 [vinyl]. Ostfildern, Germany: Intercord Record Service.

Peterkin, S. (1985). Step on the gas (Hit The Road Don) [Recorded by P. King]. [Vinyl]. London, England: Fashion Records.

Emmanuel, D. (1984). Cockney Translation [Recorded by Smiley Culture]. [Vinyl]. London, England: Fashion Records.

Emmanuel, D. (1984). Police Officer [Recorded by Smiley Culture]. [Vinyl]. London, England: Fashion Records.

Schofield, C., & Jones, B. (2019). "Whatever Community Is, This Is Not It": Notting Hill and the reconstruction of "Race" in Britain after 1958. *Journal of British Studies*, 58(1), 142–173. doi:10.1017/jbr.2018.174.

de Paor-Evans, A. (2020). *Provincial Headz: British Hip Hop and Critical Regionalism*. Equinox.

Stumer, A. (2010). *The presumption of innocence: Evidential and human rights perspectives*. Bloomsbury Publishing.

Moran, J. (2005). "Blue walls," "grey areas" and "cleanups": Issues in the control of police corruption in England and Wales. *Crime, law and social change*, 43(1), 57–79.

Channel 4 News. (2011, April). *Police "failed miserably" dead reggae star Smiley Culture*. Police "failed miserably" dead reggae star Smiley Culture—Channel 4 https://www.channel4.com/news/police-failed-miserably-dead-reggae-star-smiley-culture

BBC News. (2013, July). *Reggae star Smiley Culture stabbed himself during police raid*. https://www.bbc.co.uk/news/uk-england-23146121

GOV.UK. (2020, March). *Ethnicity facts and figures*. Stop and search—GOV.UK Ethnicity facts and figures (ethnicity-facts-figures.service.gov.uk)

Official Charts Company. (2020, March). *SMILEY CULTURE | full Official Chart History* | https://www.officialcharts.com/artist/22166/smiley-culture/

Legal Ambiguities and Cultural Power Struggles: The Moral and Legal Persecution of Rap in India

Lenard G. Gomes and Elloit Cardozo

Introduction

J. Griffith Rollefson discusses how while Hip Hop tends to be read as a marginalized "resistance vernacular" in the West, it is also a manifestly mainstream cultural commodity. Furthermore, it is an alternative form of assimilation into national discourses, languages, and economies. Despite its powerfully liberating core message then, Hip Hop—especially in its commodity forms—helps spread misogyny and homophobia while glorifying violence and celebrating materialism (Rollefson, 2017, p. 7). The public perception of Hip Hop in India exemplifies these starkly ironic extremes. Hip Hop is believed to have "arrived" in India with Baba Sehgal's rap albums in the 1990s, before non-mainstream scenes "shaped by artistic and cultural practices that are produced, defined, and sustained primarily by youth in their own neighborhoods and communities" (Morgan & Bennett, 2011, p. 180) slowly began cropping up in many cities all over India in the mid-2000s. While these scenes have steadily grown in breadth and scope, Hip Hop continues to be understood by a large part of India through its (mis)representation in mainstream music.

Despite having been around since the 1990s, it was not until the early 2010s and Yo Yo Honey Singh's rise to prominence that Hip Hop and rap became an indispensable part of mainstream music. The eventual arrival of Yo Yo Honey Singh and his former crewmates at *Mafia Mundeer*, namely Badshah, Raftaar, and Ikka in Bollywood: the Hindi-language film industry based out of Mumbai, marked a paradigm shift. Throughout the 2010s, a very specific kind of rap music continued to be perceived as what Hip Hop was representative of: the image represented by these rappers, especially in their songs for Bollywood. Parallelly, many little-known rappers from underground scenes throughout the country grew more confident with their identities and skill sets with time and there has been a surge of an "authentic" variant of Hip Hop which deals with issues immediately concerning these artistes. Despite the global praise and adulation this has garnered in the past few years, including appearances on BBC Radio and deals with global record labels, the mass perception continues to be based on the aforementioned mainstream representation of rap.

Hopefully, this is slowly beginning to change, with 2019 seeing the release of Zoya Akhtar's Bollywood blockbuster *Gully Boy* (2019), a film inspired by the stories of DIVINE and Naezy: two underground rappers from Mumbai. *Gully Boy* introduced Indian audiences to a different, more grounded, and less pompous variant of rap from the one with which they were familiar. Yet, the mass perception of rap in the country remains dismissive at best, and hostile at worst.

Early Transgressions and the Moral Persecution of Rap/e Culture in India

It is not very uncommon for the words rap and rape to be mixed up, often in jest and more so by speakers of languages other than English (Rindani, 2015, 6:06–6:12). The oft standoffish attitude towards Hip Hop and especially rap in India is not completely unjustified. Badshah and Yo Yo Honey Singh, two of the most prominent mainstream rappers who have now come to embody the mass conception of rap in the country, notoriously created shock tracks like *"Main Hoon Balatkari"* [I am a Rapist] and *"Choot Vol. 1"* [Vagina] early in their careers. These tracks were heavily criticized in the aftermath of the brutal gang-rape and murder of Jyoti Singh, on December 16, 2012, famously known as the *"Nirbhaya"* [fearless] case.

Singh's legal troubles began in the immediate aftermath of the Nirbhaya rape case in December 2012 (Biswas & Das, 2013). It is during this time that he earned the moniker "King of Rape Rap", and faced hate and criticism online in a censorious e-campaign. A First Information Report (FIR) was filed against him alleging the rapper of obscenity and inciting violence against women (Gabriel, 2016, p. 207). Singh found himself in the middle of a scandal and faced criticism when *"Main Hoon Balatkari"* and *"Choot Vol. 1"*, resurfaced on music-sharing platforms and YouTube, and began being linked to the aforementioned Nirbhaya case. These tracks came under fire for promoting rape culture and an online Petition even led to the cancellation of Singh's New Year performance at the Bristol Hotel in Gurgaon, Haryana, India (Oommen, 2013). Despite him constantly stating that the songs didn't belong to him, a criminal case was filed against Singh at the Nawanshahr police station, booking him under section 294 of the criminal law of India, also known as the Indian Penal Code (IPC). Section 294 of the code has two elements, the first singing, reciting, or repeating obscene songs and ballads and the second "to the annoyance of others" (Indian Penal Code, [1860], Act 45 of 1860). "Annoyance" here is an undefined term. The code section prescribes imprisonment up to three months for behavior and conduct that is subjective rather than objective. A deficiency in the law, the word annoyance could mean many different things. What is annoying to one may not be annoying to another, young persons loitering on the street, speaking loudly, and using crass language may "annoy" an old lady passing by, but does it necessitate or even equate to a jail sentence? The IPC section 294 is subjective for anyone interpreting, enforcing, and applying the law, meaning there is a possibility for unfair misconduct and mistreatment for those who are targeted by the "annoyance" claim that may violate their freedom of speech, conduct, or expression. In section 293 of the IPC, any material is considered obscene when it is lascivious or appeals to the prurient interests and tends to deprave and corrupt those "exposed" to the material. This is an antiquated definition of obscenity that has not been updated since the British first codified the penal laws.

Singh was also accused of singing vulgar songs laden with sexually violent content directed towards women (*Kractivist*, 2013). Shortly after, both Singh and Badshah (who featured alongside him on "*Choot Vol. 1*") saw a criminal case registered against them by the Nagpur police for obscenity-related charges under the IPC and the Information Technology Act (IT Act). The IT Act is the law regarding transmission and publication of content on the internet and the rappers Singh and Badshah were charged under it due to their alleged publication of music online. In essence, they were charged with spreading bad influence with their vulgar lyrics, especially in the light of the Nirbhaya rape case, where a 23-year-old medical student was raped and brutalized with a pipe, by a gang of men, and later died from her injuries (Hooli, 2014). Notably, despite his popularity in the mainstream, Yo Yo Honey Singh continues to be seen by many as the antithesis of "real" Hip Hop in India (Dattatreyan & Singh, 2020, p. 39), especially rap artists who are a part of the numerous underground Hip Hop scenes. "*Choot Vol. 1*" and "*Main Hoon Balatkari*", the two tracks that led to the outcry against Singh are laden with depictions of sexual violence against women and see him ramp up what he was then already infamous for: "a sort of machismo that inevitably leads to the labeling of women as either sexy or slutty. In his tracks, women are decorative… objects to be pursued… or people who get called out for stepping out of the gender lines that he assigns them" (Oommen, 2013). This is a common patriarchal ideology for men in India to be the dominant sex and to perceive women as submissive objects to obtain and conquer, which is problematic for women's overall safety and well-being.

While there exists a real threat to women's safety in India, and the cries of the victims of rape, gender violence, domestic abuse and interpersonal violence in dating relationships and marriages cannot and should not go unheard, placing the blame solely on rap and Hip Hop music is shortsighted and does not address the underlying antiquated gender roles and norms in India, let alone the systemic oppression against women. Women are still often viewed as objects: they are blamed for being victims of rape and still forced to pay dowry at marriage. Blaming Hip Hop music for such pre-existing societal woes is ignoring the actual causes of violence and does not fix the root problem, but scapegoats Hip Hop as the "cause" for gender-based violence. Besides, "Honey Singh does not exist in a vacuum; his brand of masochistic, sexist lyrical content is the norm rather than the exception" (Oommen, 2013). He is a product of his environment and cultural expectation, producing content to further reinforce gender norms in India and toxic masculinity that poses a threat to the well-being for women in India. Persecuting sexually explicit Hip Hop content is a bandage to a deep wound and only treats the symptoms, *but does not cure the deep-rooted issues in society*. In discussing the debate around censoring Yo Yo Honey Singh back in 2013, and its implications for free speech, Becky Bergdahl discusses various implementations of what she calls a "counter-speech" (2013, pp. 53–55) approach where "a government shall try to strengthen groups targeted by hate speech so that they can speak back, rather than banning hate speech in itself" (2013, p. 11) as a possible solution. However, she points out a loophole in that the Indian Penal Code only incriminates hate directed on the grounds of ethnicity, religion, and caste with gender characterized by its conspicuous absence. She even goes as far as suggesting that "[i]t is discriminatory to criminalise speech that promotes hatred against ethnic and religious groups and castes, while not criminalising similar speech directed against women" (Bergdahl, 2013, p. 43).

A criminological analysis of the Singh and Badshah case studies needs to begin with Edwin Sutherland's Social Learning Theory. Sutherland's theory of differential association says that delinquent behavior is learned from the social association in close interpersonal groups. The learned behavior can include specific techniques and methods of committing a crime and motivations and drives are learned from the excessive exposure to definitions "favorable to violation of the law" over the definitions "unfavorable to violation of law" (Sutherland, 1992). Applying Sutherland's theory of differential association, the patriarchal aggressive "male-like tendencies" which lead to delinquent and criminal behavior are taught among peers and are bred within the environmental, social, and cultural contexts of mainstream Hip Hop. Arguably, the tracks, *"Main Hoon Balatkari"* and *"Choot"* acted as catalysts to some extent to promote misogynistic ideas and a culture of rape. While the tracks did not reach mainstream audiences when released, many young people were disseminating them to close personal friends and peer groups. The songs entered the general consciousness of adolescents who considered knowing the tracks and their lyrics as "cool" and "hip". The tracks themselves are extremely explicit and maybe intentionally, inadvertently, function as instructionals for rape. It may not have been directly responsible for the uptick in the number of rape cases, especially in the north and northeastern states of the country, but this type of music has some influence on underdeveloped adolescent minds.

The hypermasculine side of Hip Hop has continued to get rappers in trouble with the law in more recent times as well. Another notable example is the incident of Sidhu Moosewala being booked under relevant sections of the IPC for promoting violence and gun culture in his track "Sanju" (*The Tribune*, 2020). This came hot on the heels of a controversy where the rapper was charged with refusing to comply with obstruction of justice that prevented an officer from carrying out their duties and firing unauthorized firearms for social media content (Sharma, 2020). The rapper then created a track discussing how his criminal offenses were not tied to his music, but was punished for having a random video online of himself with law enforcement shooting guns. This act is fairly legal and Moosewaala felt targeted because he was a rapper that sometimes creates controversial content. While not completely unjustified, Moosewaala's legal persecution for "Sanju" still does seem to stem out of preceding moral persecution as evidenced by the claims that the track is "clearly intended not only to ridicule, mock and undermine the police but also showed that the singer is incorrigible" (*The Tribune*, 2020) and that the rapper "seems to wear the FIR against him like a badge of honor" (Sethi, 2020).

The intersection of the horrific Nirbhaya case and the resurgence of Singh's early music work with overtly sexual and sexualized content seem to have made him the perfect scapegoat for public outrage and anger. However, the ambiguity in the language of the law opens the door to future prosecution of legitimate protest rappers in India. Subsequent examples in this chapter will demonstrate how the law is used to silence legitimate critiques of authority in India. Those who have a voice and choose to make it heard for potential progress for India are often ostracised and persecuted from media platforms and mistreated by the law due to its vague ambiguity. A cursory look at the work of mainstream rappers would lead one to believe that Hip Hop in India "seems to have skipped the growing-pains years of politicization that signified the 90s–era American [Hip Hop] and instead has gone straight to a flashy present, complete with expensive cars, macho lifestyles, and representations of women as objects to be used or talked down to" (Oommen, 2013). This claim however, would be off the mark, as is proved by the emergence of a more sociopolitically conscious and much more nuanced underground Hip Hop culture in the country. While the incidents discussed so far seem to have emanated from and fed the moral persecution of rap, an argument can be made that this moral persecution can come dangerously close to the suppression of political free speech, and possibly even spell a threat for more politically driven artists in the country.

Legal Ambiguities, the Suppression of Free Speech, and an Impending Cultural Power Struggle

While the previous examples stem from the problematic nature of hyper-masculinity, misogyny, and sexism in rap, there are also instances where the treatment of Hip Hop as a cultural "other" seems to have facilitated the suppression of differing opinions, effectually stifling artistic freedom, and muffling political free speech. There is a marked difference between the analyses of the case studies so far and the ones to follow. As opposed to Singh and Badshah, Babu Haabi, MC Kash and MC Kode represent the opposite spectrum of Hip Hop in India: they are predominantly underground rappers.

Every civilization throughout history has been successful because all its citizens agree with the unspoken social contract. When citizens break the social norms and no longer abide by this contract, they commit a crime. This is the most basic sociological and criminological definition of a crime. Yet, throughout history, every time there has been social progress, like the Civil Rights Movement in the U.S., the Anti-Apathied movement in South Africa, or even the Indian Independence movement, the people on the forefront are always villainized as "criminals" in the eyes of the law. Yet in all those examples, it was the law that eventually changed and not the movement. Similarly, there seems to be a slow-brewing knack for critique towards the powers-that-be in the underground rap culture in India. In 2016, the rapper Babu Haabi released a track called "Bobocanta". In the music video, he portrays M.K. Gandhi B-Boying in front of a burning Indian Parliament Building (Haabi, 2016). This visual in the music video was controversial for members of Parliament and a complaint was filed against Haabi. Charges were filed against the rapper under the following sections: 66 & 79 (spread of offensive material to incite public anger or violence), the IT Act 2000 and Sec 292 (promotion of obscenity and depravity via online media), 124A (exciting disaffection towards government), & 153A (promoting enmity between different groups with acts prejudicial to maintenance of harmony) of the IPC (Pawar, 2016). For Haabi, however, this was his interpretation of how Gandhi would react if he saw the state of affairs in the country he gave his life for. (Babu Haabi, 2016).

Section 124A of the Indian Penal Code, which defines sedition as "whoever, by words, either spoken or written, or by signs, or by visible representation, or otherwise, brings or attempts to bring into hatred or contempt, or excites or attempts to excite disaffection towards, the Government established by law in India, shall be punished by imprisonment for life" (Indian Penal Code [1860], Act 42 od 1860), while clearly providing two exceptions, namely criticism of Government measures and actions. Artistic intention aside, Haabi's depiction of Gandhi did not rise to seditious levels. In the video, he voiced his opinion on the Government and the criticism of its (in)action. Disagreeing with the Government is not seditious and depicting the parliament building burning metaphorically, in an art piece is not inciting violence. The song itself talks about the rapper's experiences and the hard work he put into his career. He describes how the system let him down and talks about his path to success. He is not advocating violence towards another group, nor is he not promoting or distributing obscene and depraved materials. The problem with vague language once again rears its head in this case. Haabi did not make a sexually explicit video, he does not have the hallmarks of a regular rap video. He has an artistic and animated depiction of Mahatma Gandhi dancing. There is no reference to any religion and the only group criticized are lawmakers, yet he is charged under the same sections of the IPC as Yo Yo Honey Singh and Badshah. If the law can be interpreted to have such diametrically opposed means, isn't there a need for it to be refreshed?

Perhaps the most riveting of these cases is when MC Kash ran into trouble during a live performance in Bengaluru (amongst numerous other occasions) where he was initially surrounded and threatened by police officers before his performance before they then cut off the sound system as soon as he got on the mic. As a rapper who proactively speaks about the political issues plaguing the border-disputed state of Kashmir, MC Kash has repeatedly been met with opposition, often by the high-handedness facilitated by the aforementioned cultural "othering" of Hip Hop. MC Kash comes from a marginalized community of the ethnic Kashmiris and he is passionate about making visible the struggle of his people. The state of Jammu and Kashmir has been the focus of many violent altercations between the Indian National Army and the National Army of Pakistan since the two countries gained Independence from the British Crown in 1947. Since then, hundreds of thousands of young innocent civilians have been caught in the crossfire. Giving voice to over seventy years of dissent, bubbling just below the surface, MC Kash dropped the protest track "I Protest" in 2014 enumerating the human rights violations and atrocities that the Indian Army committed in the Kashmir Valley. In 2016, Amnesty International of India organized an event to highlight such human rights violations in Bengaluru, and were charged with Sedition under section 124 of the IPC. Adivarekar provides an eye-witness' account of what transpired at the Amnesty event. The event started peacefully with minimal conflict from the audience, yet the Bengaluru police showed up promptly at 8:30 pm in order to terminate the event. MC Kash had only just begun performing his set and was not allowed to perform more than one track (Adivarekar, 2016). In Kash's own words, the police detained and grilled him, threatening him with jail time if they found his lyrics "anti-national" (MC Kash, 2016). Since then, MC Kash's voice is being silenced by government officials because of his outspoken controversial music that is breaking the unspoken social contract in India and questioning the status quo.

Kash, best known for "I Protest", through his lyrics shines a light on the atrocities in Kashmir valley. This video shows the real deaths and suffering caused by the military intervention and cross-border conflict that has become a sad reality for the residents and civilians of the region. He cries for his people, names the victims in his lyrics and asks for the violence to stop. As it stands today, Kashmir is a part of India, its citizens are Indian citizens. Kash is an Indian citizen, but the Indian state and the police have significantly alienated this vulnerable part of the population and is actively pursuing sedition charges, thereby silencing their own citizens' voices. Charges are brought against individuals who express opinions that bring awareness to atrocities and call for a change in leadership. Art. 19 of the Constitution protects the inherent Freedoms of speech and expression and prevents the government from infringing on such freedoms, without reason (Constitution, 1950). While the Constitution does allow the Government to impose some restrictions, in the interest of national security, safety and national sovereignty, MC Kash's statements and sentiments do not meet the threshold of endangering national security, but he poses a threat because he opposes the status quo while the government silences the voices of the people. Furthermore, built into the definition of sedition in the IPC is a provision allowing for the disapprobation, meaning strong disapproval of government actions and measures. Yet, the police officers detained and questioned Kash. This is a case study on law enforcement discretion in the face of established law, but also brings into question who interprets and enforces the law. The Bengaluru Police force had no right to detain and question MC Kash, as he was invited to the event, stayed within his bounds, and presumably followed the law. Article 19 of the Constitution protected his freedom of speech against government interference and his behavior did not rise above disapprobation of the government measures and actions as clearly enumerated in the IPC. Yet the police arrived at the venue under the guise of maintaining local noise ordinances, detained the rapper with no legal authority and then entertained a sedition complaint against the rapper and the venue. This is extra-judicial overreach on the part of the three officers of the Bengaluru Police Department. This begs the question if the police are there to protect and serve the people, or to protect and serve the government and silence the voices of those that pose a threat to the government such as MC Kash.

The most recent, and perhaps the one most emblematic of a forthcoming paradigm shift is the controversy surrounding battle rapper MC Kode. In late-May 2021, the Delhi-based battle rapper and organizer found himself on the receiving end of relentless online abuse over the resurfacing of an almost five-year-old video where he is seen and heard dishing out unpleasantries about Hindu religious texts. The resurfacing of this video, thanks to an online Meme Page named Yo Yo Bantai Rapstar, that also spurred on detractors, led to MC Kode falling victim to the recent upsurge of "cancel culture": "the withdrawal of any kind of support (viewership, social media follows, purchases of products endorsed by the person, etc.) for those who are assessed to have said or done something unacceptable or highly problematic, generally from a social justice perspective" (Ng, 2020, p. 623). Kode was forced to take down all of his work from the internet and lost as many as nine brand endorsements (*Free Press Journal*, 2021), amidst the downpour of harassment, death threats, and calls for legal action against him (Bailoor, 2021). This incident, especially if the unconfirmed reports of an FIR being filed leading to his arrest hold any credence, are indicative of much larger systemic issues. The concept of cancel culture can emerge online to suppress the artistry and voiced opinion of artists as an online form of non-state policing of what is acceptable and what is not on the world wide web.

One of the first criticisms against MC Kode is the cultural imperialism underlying the out-of-context interpretation of the video, which comes from a fundamental lack of understanding of the battle rap culture. It is important to understand that battle rap is essentially a form of verbal duelling that offers rappers "the possibility both to praise one's own qualities (boastin') and to weaken the reputation of the opponent, e.g., by questioning his/her technical skills, his/her sexual power, and the personal integrity of the rapper or his/her mother's personal integrity (dissin')" (Kautny, 2015, p. 112). In a duel where the participating rappers' sole aim is to one-up their opponent, insults, gestures and disrespect are often fired with the intention of humiliating the opponent. What is significant here, is that the person being humiliated is complicit, and the entire act of battle rapping is very performative. For a comparison, thinking of what is said in a battle rap as an insult to anyone except the involved rappers is like accusing martial artists of physical assault: "[b]attlers often hover and circle each other as if they were mixed martial arts fighters, attacking each other with words instead of punches and kicks" (Bacon, 2018, p. 8). It is very clear hence, that the abuse directed towards MC Kode comes not only from a lack of context but also from a lack of understanding of the battle rap culture in Hip Hop. The second of these implicitly systemic issues is the process of establishing the cultural "otherness" of Hip Hop: "the result of a discursive process by which a dominant in-group ("Us," the Self) constructs one or many dominated out-groups ("Them," Other) by stigmatizing a difference –real or imagined –presented as a negation of identity and thus a motive for potential discrimination [and/ or subjugation]" (Staszak, 2009, p. 43). Infamously associated with aggressive traits such as rape culture since the early half of the 2010s, rap music became a convenient scapegoat to pin everything that was "deviant" upon a culture that came in from "foreign" shores. This "otherness" of Hip Hop constructed by a discourse of cultural vigilantism in India blames social issues of misogyny and sexism almost entirely upon Hip Hop.

Conclusion

This cultural heavy-handedness implicit in the treatment of rap seems to be indicative of an impending power struggle, where anything deemed "uncultured", against the established social norms gets subjected to legal persecution on grounds of being "offensive". What is actually offensive is the unspoken societal norms and social contract that continue to encourage the patriarchal, sexist, and abusive views towards women, without true pathways toward healing. What is actually offensive is the choice to scapegoat Hip Hop, versus truly making progressive holistic pathways towards healing and resolution for marginalized oppressed people in India. Finally, what is actually more offensive is the silencing of voices of the people who are protesting their oppression and need for societal change through music rather than actually listening and responding to their voices. There needs to be a revision of the vague policies of the IPC with more clearer definitions for law enforcement to abide in the best interest for the people of India. There needs to be more cooperation for the government to work with progressive artists that question the status quo and to be more malleable towards the needs and listen to the recommendations of its citizens.

Acknowledgments

The authors thank Devanjali Banerjee for her contribution to the ideation of the early stages of this chapter. They also express their gratitude to Marissa Denay Rodriguez for her feedback during the writing of the chapter. Cardozo also thanks and appreciates the Panchtatva crew for helping him keep up-to-steam with recent happenings in the underground Hip Hop scenes.

References

Adivarekar, H. (2016, August 16). "Things got heated but not threatening": An eyewitness account of Amnesty's contentious Kashmir meet. *Scroll.in*. https://scroll.in/article/814150/things-got-heated-but-not-threatening-an-eyewitness-account-of-amnestys-contentious-kashmir-meet

Babu Haabi. (2016, September 20). "I Am Getting Threatening Calls": Babu Haabi. *Bollywood Hungama*. [Video]. https://www.bollywoodhungama.com/videos/celeb-interviews/i-am-getting-threatening-calls-babu-haabi/

Bacon, E. T. (2018). Between live performance and mediated narrative: Contemporary rap battle culture in context. In J. D. Burton & J. L. Oakes (Eds.), *The Oxford handbook of Hip Hop music* (pp. 1–19). Oxford Handbooks Online. https://www.oxfordhandbooks.com/view/10.1093/oxfordhb/9780190281090.001.0001/oxfordhb-9780190281090

Bailoor, G. (2021, May 30). Battle rap in Digital India: The Artists vs. The Arbiters. *Rolling Stone India*. https://rollingstoneindia.com/battle-rap-mc-kode-right-wing-doxxed/

Bergdahl, B. (2013). *Yo ban? Rape rap and limits of free speech in India: An argument analysis of the debate about banning the artist Honey Singh* (Master's thesis). https://www.diva-portal.org/smash/record.jsf?pid=diva2%3A625220&dswid=-237

Biswas, T. (2013, July 13). Delhi gang-rape case: What happened that night. (M. Das, Ed.) *NDTV*. https://www.ndtv.com/delhi-news/delhi-gang-rape-case-what-happened-that-night-508293

Constitution of India. (1950). https://legislative.gov.in/constitution-of-india

Dattatreyan, E. G., & Singh, J. N. (2020). Ciphers, 'hoods and digital DIY studios in India: Negotiating aspirational individuality and Hip-Hop collectivity. *Global Hip-Hop Studies*, *1*(1), 25–45. https://doi.org/10.1386/ghhs_00003_1

Gabriel, K. (2016). Sexuality, mediation, commodification: The business of representation. In R. Ramdev, S. D. Nambiar, & D. Bhattacharya (Eds.), *Sentiment, politics, censorship: The state of hurt* (pp. 207–223). New Delhi: SAGE.

Hooli, S. H. (2014, December 30). Yo Yo Honey Singh, Badshah in Legal Problem; Delhi, Nagpur Police on Look-out for Rappers. *IB Times*. https://www.ibtimes.co.in/yo-yo-honey-singh-badshah-legal-problem-delhi-nagpur-police-look-out-rappers-618770

Indian Penal Code, [1860], Act 45 of 1860. https://www.iitk.ac.in/wc/data/IPC_186045.pdf

Kautny, O. (2015). Lyrics and flow in rap music. In J. A. Williams (Ed.), *The Cambridge companion to hip-hop* (pp. 111–126). Cambridge University Press.

MC Kash. (2016, August 20). "Heart of a Rebel": Kashmiri Rapper MC Kash narrates his Banglore Ordeal. *Kashmirlife.net*. https://kashmirlife.net/heart-of-a-rebel-kashmiri-rapper-mc-kash-narrates-his-bangalore-ordeal-115282/

Morgan, M. G., & Bennett, D. (2011). Hip-Hop & the global imprint of a black cultural form. *Daedalus*, *140*(2), 176–196. https://doi.org/10.1162/DAED_a_00086

Ng, E. (2020). No grand pronouncements here...: Reflections on cancel culture and digital media participation. *Television & New Media*, *21*(6), 621–627. https://doi.org/10.1177/1527476420918828

Oommen, I. K. (2013). Bitter honey: Sexual violence in Desi Hip-Hop. *Jaggery: A DesiLit Arts and Literature Journal*, (1). http://jaggerylit.com/issue-1-fall-2013/bitter-honey-sexual-violence-in-desi-hip-hop/.

Pawar, Y. (2016, September 11). Complaint against rapper Babu Haabi for "insulting" Gandhi and Parliament. *DNA*. https://www.dnaindia.com/india/report-complaint-against-rap-star-babu-haabi-for-insulting-gandhi-and-parliament-2253955

Punjabi singer Sidhu Moosewala booked for promoting violence, gun culture in new song "Sanju". (2020, July 20). *The Tribune*. https://www.tribuneindia.com/news/punjab/another-case-registered-against-punjabi-singer-sidhu-moosewala-115428

Rapper MC Kode under fire for abusing Hinduism in old rap battle video; issues apology (2021, May 27). *Free Press Journal*. https://www.freepressjournal.in/viral/rapper-mc-kode-under-fire-for-abusing-hinduism-in-old-rap-battle-video-issues-apology

Rindani, D. N. (Director). (2015). *Bombay 70 – Mami '14 Best Short Film*. YouTube: Triangular Motion Pictures. https://www.youtube.com/watch?v=WmC4elJcICA&ab_channel=TriangularMotionPictures

Rollefson, J. G. (2017). *Flip the script: European hip-hop and the politics of postcoloniality*. Chicago; London: The University of Chicago Press.

Sethi, C. K. (2020, July 20). Rapper Sidhu Moosewala booked for promoting violence after he hails Arms Act FIR in song. *The Print*. https://theprint.in/india/rap

per-sidhu-moosewala-booked-for-promoting-violence-after-he-hails-arms-act-fir-in-song/464910/

Sharma, P. (2020, June 30). Punjabi singer Sidhu Moosewala gets interim bail in Sangrur FIR. *The Tribune.* https://www.tribuneindia.com/news/punjab/punjabi-singer-sidhu-moosewala-gets-interim-bail-in-sangrur-fir-106681

Sutherland, E. H., Cressey, D. R., & Luckenbill, D. F. (1992). *Principles of criminology.* Altamira Press.

Staszak, J.-F. (2009). Other/Otherness. In *International encyclopedia of human geography* (Vol. 8, pp. 43–47). Elsevier.

Vulgar Song Case: Fir Filed Against Punjabi Rapper Honey Singh. (2013, May 17). *Kractivist.* https://www.kractivist.org/vulgar-song-case-fir-filed-against-punjabi-rapper-honey-singh/

Afterword

TASHA IGLESIAS

Although I grew up with Tupac and Biggie on the radio and television, I did not fully understand the Hip Hop culture until I began attending breakin' jams (breakdancing competitions) in Southern California. It was in these spaces that I saw the love within the culture, and began to make connections between leadership strategies and effective pedagogies used in educational spaces, and those taught and learned within Hip Hop culture. As a graduate student wanting to study Hip Hop, it was difficult to articulate why participants needed to unlearn what they knew about Hip Hop and instead see the value of this culture. As I began to grow my network through Hip Hop culture and academia, learn more about effective interventions and new research being published, I gained more confidence in my ability to both represent and advocate on behalf of the culture in educational and organizational settings.

Training faculty, teachers, admin and staff about a culture I belonged to proved to be more difficult than expected; many of my participants did not know about the culture beyond what they heard on the radio and viewed on television. They, like wider society, saw Hip Hop as a negative force on the youth, one which glamorized sexism, materialism and violence. The book *Beats Not Beatings: The Rise of Hip Hop Criminology* (2024) explores both the criminalization of Hip Hop, but also the hypocrisies surrounding these perceptions. *Beats Not Beatings: The Rise of Hip Hop Criminology* (2024) also does something else, it highlights the beauty of this culture and its potential to empower and transform lives, a concept that is often overlooked because of the associated bias and prejudice.

Ward (2024) explains that Hip Hop has been, since its creation, "subject to scrutiny and even criminalization from those in power" (p. xviii). Part of the reason for this demonization and scrutiny is because "…opposes the status quo while the government silences the voices of the people" (Gomes & Cardozo, 2024, p. 98). Since the beginning, Hip Hop has spoken out about institutional and individual discrimination and racism and the role of the government in keeping people in poverty. Gomes and Cardozo (2024) explain that "Blaming Hip Hop music for such pre- existing societal woes is ignoring the actual causes of violence and does not fix the problem, but scapegoats Hip Hop as the 'cause' for gender based violence" (2024, p. 94). In other words, as Crenshaw (2024) argues, Hip Hop "is just a reflection of the larger society and its values" (p. xiii?); Hip Hop is a voice of the marginalized, and underrepresented (Graham-Bey et al., 2024) and speaks loudly against social inequalities like structural racism (Paor, Evans, 2024). Because of my engagement in this culture; I knew about real Hip Hop, I knew Hip Hop prioritized self-love and love-of-others above anything else.

Hip Hop is a culture with core values that include peace, love, unity and having fun. Dr. Bettina Love (2015) explains that "…the culture of Hip Hop is present in the lives of young children, beyond just the element of rap, which is why [Hip Hop Based Education] is important to the field" (p. 108). As scholars continue to study the impact of Hip Hop on marginalized communities, they find that Hip Hop's values and pedagogical methods can be used beyond the field of education and Hip Hop as a culture is truly interdisciplinary. Graham-Bey et al. (2013) explains that "Hip Hop is a culture; a lifestyle; something that we must take into strong consideration and begin to not just analyze it for lyrical purposes, but begin to ask, what does and can Hip Hop offer theologically and how it might inform our own lives? (p. 3).

I would argue that Hip Hop is woven into the fabric of our lives and this culture not only informs how we view and respond to the world, but also pushes us as individuals to be the best authentic versions of ourselves. Hodge (2024) explores this concept when describing his connection to Hip Hop. Hodge (2023) explains that Hip Hop made him feel like his own "identity was validated in the music and that it was 'okay' to be [himself]" (p. 1?). Knowledge of the culture, and knowledge of one's self is "at the core essence of the hip hop culture" (de Paor-Evans, 2024, p. 108) and can be applied to all communities experiencing trauma, who belong to marginalized communities, or just need to be celebrated. Hip Hop has the ability to transform lives; either through its music (Mendoza, 2024), through its advocacy and ability to empower vulnerable communities (Crenshaw, 2024) or through its lyrics. It is not surprising to see how Hip Hop can allow those imprisoned to value themselves while also knowing there is a culture who will accept them

Afterword

as they are and support them as they realize the best version of their authentic self. Sulé (2016) reiterates this value of Hip Hop by stating Hip Hop gives people "a sense of mattering, but also [provides] opportunities to understand how others mattered" (p. 108). In other words, Hip Hop shows vulnerable populations that they matter, and also inspires them to uphold Hip Hop's tenets at the same time; peace, love, unity and having fun; themes similar to restorative justice and pathways to healing in the criminal justice system.

Lastly, Hip Hop creates a sense of belonging through its crews; a family based on a shared mission rather than confined to biological ties. These crews are often lead by the pioneers or OGs who are, as Crenshaw (2024) explains, "not rich and famous, [but] are contributing and bringing value to the culture because they love it and it is empowering" (Crenshaw, 2024, p. xiv?). Hip Hop educators, artivists, leaders and members are loyal to their crews and the culture and often prioritize mentorship when teaching and leading the youth. Members are accepted as they are and celebrated for their authentic selves. Their struggles are not minimized and rather than pass judgment, OGs help develop the crew member's navigational and resistant capital (Yosso, 2005). "Together, esteem, resilience, growth, community, and change are core values of Hip Hop culture-values that give the culture direction and purpose" (Travis, 2015, p. 108).

Culton (2024) explained that "Skateboarders go where they shouldn't, and they do things that were unintended" (p. 26). Hip Hop has gone where it shouldn't go and critiqued structural racism and instructional discrimination despite being demonized and criminalized. In reality, Hip Hop does quite the opposite, like the stories highlighted in this book, *Beats Not Beatings: The Rise of Hip Hop Criminology (2024)*, it provides a voice to the voiceless and a family to those who need and should be accepted for their authentic self. Hip Hop provides a space to heal and work through trauma and develop resilience and perseverance when becoming the best version of themselves. In some ways, Hip Hop is seeking to go where it is needed in both educational and organizational settings. The use of Hip Hop in non-traditional or academic settings is still in development and has much more work that needs to be done, including becoming more accepting and inclusive of other cultures and marginalized groups like the LGBTQ population (Hunt & Rhodes, 2024, p. 108) and those with disabilities. In the end, those in the culture are well aware of its power to transform lives and help many heal, we just need to help wider society unlearn what they know about Hip Hop and instead see a culture full of love.

References

Crenshaw, M. (2024). Foreword. In A. J. Nocella II (Ed.), *Beats not beatings: The rise of hip hop criminology*. Peter Lang Publishing.

Culton, K. R. (2024). Next-level postmodernism and the presentation of realness in hip-hop. In A. J. Nocella II (Ed.), *Beats not beatings: The rise of hip hop criminology*. Peter Lang Publishing.

de Paor-Evans, A. (2024). Stop and search: Representations of police harassment in British hip-hop during the 1980s. In A. J. Nocella II (Ed.), *Beats not beatings: The rise of hip hop criminology*. Peter Lang Publishing.

Graham-Bey, R. Hodge, D. W., Nocella, A. J., & Quintana, A. (2024). Introduction. *Beats not beatings: The rise of hip hop criminology*. Peter Lang Publishing.

Gomes, L. G., & Cardozo, E. (2024). Legal Ambiguities and Cultural Power Struggles: The Moral and Legal Persecution of Rap in India. In A. J. Nocella II (Ed.), *Beats not beatings: The rise of hip hop criminology*. Peter Lang Publishing.

Hunt, A. N., & Rhodes, T. D. (2024). "No homo": Hip-hop, homophobia, and queer justice. In A. J. Nocella II (Ed.), *Beats not beatings: The rise of hip hop criminology*. Peter Lang Publishing.

Love, L. B. (2015). What is hip-hop-based education doing in nice fields such as early childhood and elementary education?. *Urban Education, 50*(1), 106–131.

Mendoza, V. (2024). Música y Libertad. In A. J. Nocella II (Ed.), *Beats not beatings: The rise of hip hop criminology*. Peter Lang Publishing.

Sule, T. (2016). Hip-hop is healer: Sense of belonging and diversity among hip-hop collegians. *Journal of College Student Development, 57*(2), 181–196.

Travis, R. (2015). *The healing power of hip hop*. Praeger.

Ward, C. (2024). Preface. In A. J. Nocella II (Ed.), *Beats not beatings: The rise of hip hop criminology*. Peter Lang Publishing.

Yosso, T. J. (2005). Whose culture has capital? *Race, Ethnicity and Education, 8*(1), 69–91.

Contributors' Biographies

Elloit Cardozo is a fellow at Maulana Abul Kalam Azad Institute of Asian Studies in Kolkata, India. He teaches the module on hip hop and research for University of Mumbai's certificate in "Introduction to Hip-Hop studies" course.

"Mic" Crenshaw was born and raised in Chicago and Minneapolis and currently resides in Portland Oregon. Crenshaw is an independent Hip Hop artist, respected emcee, poet, educator and activist. Crenshaw is the Lead U.S. Organizer for the Afrikan HipHop Caravan and uses Cultural Activism as a means to develop international solidarity related to Human Rights and Justice through Hip Hop and Popular Education. In addition to his highly-acclaimed work in spoken work and Hip Hop, Mic co-founded GlobalFam, a non-profit (EducationWithOut Borders 501c3) project to create and maintain a computer center for disadvantaged youth in Burundi, Central Africa. Mic has released numerous albums available on most popular digital platforms and has toured internationally in Tanzania, Kenya, South Africa, Zimbabwe, Russia, Germany and Cuba. Crenshaw was voted Portland's Best Hip Hop Artist in 2016 by Willamette Week. In 2019 Mic Crenshaw received the Fields Artist Fellowship Award from the Oregon Community Foundation.

Kenneth R. Culton, Ph.D, is an associate professor of sociology at Niagara University near Niagara Falls, New York. He has been a long-time participant in various music scenes as a performing musician and features a course entitled "Youth/Music/Subculture," which explores music subcultures and scenes and their potential as catalysts for social change. He is particularly interested in Hip-Hop as a space of resistance and meaning making. Other research interests include social theory, cultural sociology, and the sociology of religion and non-religion.

Lenard G. Gomes, Esq. is a criminal justice scholar and an immigration attorney licensed to practice law in the State of New York, United States. While his primary practice is immigration and family law, he has also done research in domestic violence and other criminal justice issues. In June 2020, he graduated from the John Jay College of Criminal Justice in New York, NY, with a Master's Degree in Criminal Justice. He is a member of Alpha Phi Sigma, the National Criminal Justice Honor Society of the United States.

Maurece Graham-Bey is a multilingual individual with an educational background in criminal justice, English, finance, Christian counseling, and alcohol & drug treatment. He has dedicated his life to helping people who are affected by the dysfunctional system. After his encounter with homelessness and the criminal justice system as a youth, he has become a leadership development mentor, non-violent communication and alternative to violence training facilitator, trauma & healing circle lead, Restorative living lead practitioner, Peer recovery coach, Housing navigator and advocate, and organizer for transformative justice. His work on models for addressing homelessness has influenced policies in both Seattle and Los Angeles and earned him a position as an authority on housing justice. He currently resides in Seattle and sits on the boards of the Alternatives to Violence Project, Friends for a Nonviolent World, and Projects for a Civil Society. He is currently the Co-Director of Transformative Justice with Save the Kids.

Daniel White Hodge, Ph.D., is an author, Hip Hop scholar, cultural critic, & diversity & inclusion, expert. Dr. Hodge has taught at Cal State University Northridge's Religious Studies department, Cal State Los Angeles' Pan African Studies department, as well as Fuller Theological Seminary's school of intercultural studies. As a speaker, writer, and activist he has spoken on many college campuses including Stanford University, UCLA, USC, and Union Theological Seminary. He teaches around the world on subjects such as Black popular culture, personality, and the self, Hip Hop discourse, and race/ethnicity within religion. Dr. Hodge consults and is available to speak on a variety of subjects including Hip Hop theology, race & ethnicity in the trump era, colonization in evangelicalism, & intercultural communication.

Andrea N. Hunt, Ph.D., is an Associate Professor of Sociology and the Director of the Center for Social Inclusion at the University of North Alabama. She teaches classes on inequality, hip-hop culture, and family diversity. Dr. Hunt is a violence prevention educator and works with adjudicated youth. She spends much of her time in the community engaged in program development and assessment. Her research focuses on the relationship between social media and violence; representation of gender, sexuality, disability, and race in the media; and the influence of hip-hop on the development of gendered and racialized identities in early adulthood.

Tasha Iglesias, Ph.D. currently serves as a Lecturer in the School of Education, for the University of California, Riverside, and Southern New Hampshire University. Dr. Iglesias earned a Doctorate in Educational Leadership (Ed.D) at California State University Long Beach and teaches in the Education and Social Sciences field. Dr. Iglesias's dissertation was titled "Each One, Teach One": The Impact of a Hip Hop Learning Community on the Cultural Wealth of Foster Youth in Higher Education. Dr. Iglesias's research interests include: Culturally Sustaining Pedagogy, Hip Hop Pedagogy and Praxis, and the history of Hip Hop as a culture. Dr. Iglesias develops curriculum, trains professors, consults with organizations and educational institutions and presents her research across the world. Outside of academia, Iglesias serves as the President of the Hip Hop Association of Advancement and Education (HHAAE) and Chair of the Global Conference on Hip Hop Education.

Victor Mendoza earned an Associate's—Law Enforcement Forensics (Odessa College, 2015); Bachelors—Homeland Security (Sul Ross State University, 2017); Masters—Criminal Justice (Sul Ross State University, 2019) and currently a PhD candidate—Administration of Justice (Texas Southern University). McNair Scholar (2017–2018) who presented at McNair, American Society of Criminology and American Criminal Justice Society conferences on crimmigration, prisons and criminological theory. Former member of African Criminology Society, Convict Criminology Society, currently employed at Texas Department of Transportation and over 25 years' experience with Texas Department of Corrections/Criminal Justice—Institutional/Pardons & Parole Divisions.

Anthony J. Nocella II, Ph.D., scholar-activist, is an Associate Professor in the Department of Criminal Justice in the Institute of Public Safety at Salt Lake Community College. He is the editor of the Peace Studies Journal, Transformative Justice Journal, and co-editor of five book series including Critical Animal Studies and Theory with Lexington Books and Hip Hop Studies and Activism with Peter Lang Publishing. He is the National Director of Save the Kids and Executive Director of the Institute for Critical Animal Studies. He has published over fifty book chapters or articles and forty books. He has been interviewed by New York Times, Washington Post, Houston Chronicles, Fresno Bee, Fox, CBS, CNN, C-SPAN, and Los Angeles Times.

Adam de Paor-Evans, Ph.D., ethnomusicologist and spatio-material theorist, was formerly Reader in Ethnomusicology within the Faculty of Culture and Creative Industries at UCLan, and now teaches in the School of Art, Design and Architecture at University of Plymouth. He also leads the research project: *RHYTHM OBSCURA: Revealing Hidden Histories through Ethnomusicology, Practice Research and Material Culture*. He is interested in the relationships between the intersections, intertextuality and intangibility of music cultures, their reifications, artefacts, personal histories, and representational devices. He has published three books entitled: *HIP HOP IN THE STICKS: A Deepening Con/Text* (2023), *PROVINCIAL HEADZ: British Hip Hop and Critical Regionalism* (2020), and *SCRATCHING THE SURFACE: Hip Hop, Remoteness, and Everyday Life* (2020), which intersect ethnomusicology, cultural context, and personal histories. He is also editor of HEADZ-zINe, a scholarly bi-annual hip hop zine with a critical edge.

andré douglas pond cummings J.D., is Dean Designate, Widener University Commonwealth Law School, Associate Dean for Faculty Development and Charles C. Baum Distinguished Professor of Law at the University of Arkansas at Little Rock William H. Bowen School of Law where he teaches Business Associations, Contracts I and II, Corporate Justice, Entertainment Law, Hip Hop & the American Constitution and related courses. Dean cummings also co-directs the Center for Racial Justice and Criminal Justice Reform. Additionally, cummings was Professor of Law at the West Virginia University College of Law. Before embarking on his academic career, cummings worked as a judicial law clerk for Chief Judge Joseph W. Hatchett of the United States Court of Appeals for the Eleventh Circuit and for Justice Christine M. Durham of the Utah Supreme Court. In addition, he worked at the Chicago, IL based law firm of Kirkland & Ellis LLP, focusing his practice on complex business transactions including mergers, acquisitions, divestitures and securities offerings of publicly traded corporations. Simultaneously, cummings represented clients in the sports and entertainment industries, including athletes in the National Football League, record labels, motion picture production companies, and a variety of authors, including Hollywood screenwriters. cummings writes extensively on issues regarding investor protection, racial and social justice, and sports and entertainment law, publishing in the *Washington University Law Review, Indiana Law Journal, Utah Law Review, Tulane Law Review, Howard Law Journal, Drexel Law Review, Marquette Sports Law Review, Iowa Journal of Gender, Race and Justice, Thurgood Marshall Law Review* and *Harvard Journal on Racial and Ethnic Justice*, amongst many others. cummings has published three books including "Corporate Justice" (with Todd Clark) in 2016, "Hip Hop and the Law" (with Pamela Bridgewater and Donald Tibbs) in 2015, and "Reversing Field: Examining Commercialization, Labor, Gender, and Race in 21st Century Sports Law" (with Anne Marie Lofaso) in 2010.

Antonio Quintana is a loving father, educator, emcee, and activist. He has worked in Health Promotion/Disease Prevention for over nine years, and has managed health education programs on a wide variety of topics including HIV, diabetes, fitness and nutrition. As an emcee and show promoter, Tony (also known by his stage name I.Q. the Professor) has been very active in the local hip-hop scene in Albuquerque, NM where he co-founded the Conscious Eating and Hip-Hop event series, and is a co-founder of the Dezert Banditz hip-hop crew. He is currently the Plant-Based Eating Program Manager for Animal Protection of New Mexico and Youth Education Director for the Albuquerque Center for Spiritual Living.

Tammy D. Rhodes is the Director of First Year Experience, Academic Advising & Academic Support in the University Success Center at the University of North Alabama and a doctoral student at Nova Southeastern University in Fort Lauderdale, FL. Her work focuses on retention of academically at-risk students specializing in first generation minority students. Her research interests include student success initiatives, academic advising for exploratory students, and first and second year programming in higher education. She has developed programming on the political culture of the U.S., the school to prison pipeline, body image, race relations, and anti-hazing initiatives in fraternal organizations.

Chandra Ward, Ph.D., is an Assistant Professor of Sociology at the University of Tennessee at Chattanooga teaching urban sociology and a number of other sociological topics. Her research is guided by the philosophy of helping to amplify traditionally marginalized voices. This is evident in her research on public housing residents and her textbook, an intersectional introduction to sociology reader titled, Voices From the Margin: Fresh perspectives on an introduction to sociology." Professor Ward also uses photography and social media to help make sociology accessible to those outside of academia. It can be found here at sociologysocialshutter.blogspot.com.

Index

A

Anti-Fascist 81

B

B Boys xiii
B Girls xiii
Biggie 7, 105
Bitches 31
Black Liberation 6
Blackness xvi, 4

C

California 25, 105, 111
Civilization xi, 3, 96
Civil Rights 96
Civil War 67
Classical Music 72
Criminology xvii, 5, 13, 17, 70–71, 75–76, 105, 107, 111
Critical animal studies 6, 111

D

Dance 25, 29, 31, 67, 73, 81, 83–84
Dancehall 83–84, 87–88

Death 69, 87–88, 98–99
Delinquent 94–95
Democracy 7, 40
DJ Kool Herc 2
Dogtown 25
Domestic Violence 110
Dominant xi, xiii, 6, 12, 10, 24, 27–28, 38, 94, 100

E

Eminem 40
Ethnicity 74, 94, 110

F

Feire, P. 6

G

Gangster xv, 2, 7
Genocide xi
Graffiti xiii, xvi, 27, 39, 73, 81

H

Hip Hop Education 111

Index

Hip Hop Pedagogy 4, 111
Hodge, D. W. 1, 105–106, 111
Hollywood xii, 112
Homophobic 7, 9–10, 31

I

Ice Cube 41, 44–45
Illegal 4, 39, 84
Indigenous 3, 6–7, 74

J

Jay-Z 40
Jazz 72

K

Kane, Big Daddy 10
KRS-One 3, 39, 41, 44, 46

L

Lil Nas X 15
Love xii–xiii, 1, 3, 10, 15, 25, 33, 46, 68, 87, 105–107

M

Mandela, N. 7
Marxian 24
Masculine 9, 15, 16, 32–33, 95
MC Hammer xv
MC Kash 96–99
Misogyny xi, 6, 41, 50, 91, 96, 100
Murder 29, 49, 92

N

Nocella II, A. J. 1, 3–4, 6, 111
Nuclear War 82

O

Obama, Barack 4, 40

P

Peace ix, 6–7, 111
Pedophiles 47
Pimp(ing)(s) xii
Police 39, 42–45, 50, 74, 79–80, 82–88
Police Brutality xv, 3, 6, 43, 45, 79–80, 82–83, 85, 93, 95, 97–99
Poverty 47, 48, 106
Prison 24, 37, 43–50, 71, 75–76, 88, 111
Prison Abolition(ist)(s) 76

Q

Queer 5, 9–21, 32

R

Racial Justice 112
Rapist(s) 43, 47, 92
Republican 67
Restorative Justice 75, 107
Rose, Tricia 1, 3
Russia xiii, 109

S

Sawyer III, D. C. 1
Sexism 11, 13, 96, 100, 105
Sexuality xii, 10, 14–15, 31, 111
Shakur, Tupac 41, 45, 105
Skateboard(ing) 5, 23, 25–28, 33, 107
Slavery 75, 80
Slutty 94
Social Justice 6, 40, 42, 99

T

Terrorism 3

Index

Transformative Justice ix, 6, 110–111
Trump, Donald 4, 110
Turntablist(s) xiii

V

Violence 9–14, 16–18, 26, 31–32, 39, 41, 48, 50, 91–95, 97–98, 105–106, 110–111

W

War 3, 45, 48
white supremacist xii, 4, 70, 73, 75–76

Y

Young Jeezy 40

Hip Hop Studies and Activism

Edited by
Dr. Anthony J. Nocella II
Dr. Daniel White Hodge
Dr. Don C. Sawyer
Dr. Ahmad R. Washington
Dr. Arash Daneschzadeh

Hip Hop Studies and Activism is the first book series dedicated to hip hop studies. This series is an intersectional, interdisciplinary, liberatory project that promotes justice, equity, and inclusion. *Hip Hop Studies and Activism* will connect with a broad range of disciplines such as feminism, globalization, economics, science, history, environmental studies, media studies, political science, sociology, religion, anthropology, philosophy, education, and cultural studies. Against apolitical scholarship, Hip Hop Studies argue for an engaged critical praxis that promotes a listening and defending space and place for marginalized and silenced communities, especially Communities of Color and Youth of Color. While other book series are more rooted in theory and apolitical analysis, this series is committed to social action, advocacy, and activism. We make a strong effort to publish work by and of People and Youth of Color.

To order other books in this series, please contact our Customer Service Department:
 peterlang@presswarehouse.com (within the U.S.)
 orders@peterlang.com (outside the U.S.)

Or browse online by series:
 www.peterlang.com